MODERN SCRIPTURE

TRUTH ALWAYS WINS

Abhishek

INDIA • SINGAPORE • MALAYSIA

ISBN 979-8-88869-338-4

Wishing everyone to find the truth in God, person, love, friendship and society, the basic element of life, and follow the path of truth, leading the people to live in the path of truth…

Time of writing

24/05/2011 - 24/5/2015

Contents

Part One
God

Part Two

Person

Part Three
Love, Friendship

Part Four
Society

This scripture is the
Way that tells the truth,
Truth that gives life, and
Life that contains the way.

God likes the truth

Truth is the source of God's ways.

Where there is no truth,

The paths of God become religions,

Stories become Vedas,

Inequity becomes virtue,

Intelligence becomes knowledge,

Necessity becomes love,

Dishonesty becomes ability,

Deception becomes the path,

Dark powers become the official powers,

Finally, that place becomes displeasing to God.

PART ONE

GOD

-1-

Truth, Untruth, True, Lie, Wisdom, Ignorance, Knowledge, Virtue, Theory

1. The thought that does not change according to season, place and situation is Truth.
2. It is enough if truth lets one live.

   It is enough if one person lets the truth live.
3. That which continues with untruth is dark life.

   That which continues with truth is a life of lights.
4. Those who think what they know is the truth are worthless.

   Blessed are those who know the truth.
5. Truth is not limited to a few people.

   Truth is not that, which applies to only a few people.
6. Life of those who accept the truth will be happy.

   Life of those who follow the truth is also great.
7. Truth is not that comes or is known to a human by birth. One has to know that truth at some stage.
8. Showing disobedience to the truth, rejecting the truth and acting against the truth are sinful features.
9. Treading the path of truth means knowing, obeying and following the true ones.
10. Truth can make a person independent, holy and righteous.
11. People who know the truth are equal to those who are awakened.

    People who do not know the truth are equal to those who are sleeping.

12. If there is no truth in a book, it cannot become a holy book. Likewise, it cannot be of God.
13. Those who live beyond truth do not belong to God.
14. These are able to give freedom and independence:

    1. Truth. 2. Soul.
15. That which releases from every bondage – truth.
16. That which can never be a superstition – truth.
17. Where there is no truth, there is no peace and answer.
18. The value will come to a person according to the truth. The value will not come to the truth according to a person.
19. Knowing the truth reveals the untruth.
20. Untruth will be created by ignorance and opportunism.
21. Those who live beyond truth do not like the truth.
22. Those who believe untruth and believe the truth as untruth are ignorant fools. Those who want to change untruth as truth and truth as untruth are cruel.
23. Change with violence is temporary. Change with truth is permanent.
24. True can be a lie; a lie can be true. But truth cannot be untruth; untruth cannot be the truth.
25. True and lie will change. Truth and untruth are will not change.
26. All that can be seen are true, but all that can be seen are not truth.
27. Truth and untruth are permanent. True and lie are Ephemeral.
28. That which is present now – True. That which stays forever – Truth.
29. True – Temporary, Truth – Permanent.
30. Truth does not require a proof but a lie requires a proof.
31. Truth is the answer to truth; it does not have many answers.

32. Truth is permanent, sacred, strong and powerful.
33. Thought of God – Knowledge.
34. Science belongs to humans; wisdom belongs to God. Science will change; wisdom will not change.
35. If God teaches you – wisdom. If you learn for yourself – common sense.
36. Wisdom will be a source of change, wisdom does not change.
37. Wisdom is gained from God and soul.
38. Wisdom is –

    1. You knowing yourself.

    2. That you know by yourself.
39. You will know wisdom from quotes and statements. You will gain wisdom from the soul, God and exertion.
40. The way to gain wisdom is to have fear of God and a relationship with God.
41. Two types of thoughts occur in humans:

    1. Thoughts with wisdom.

    2. Thoughts with intelligence.
42. Intelligence is of two types:

    1. Intelligence with ignorance.

    2. Intelligence with wisdom.
43. Intelligence – temporary, wisdom – permanent.
44. Change with intelligence – temporary.

    Change with wisdom – revolutionary.
45. Virtue is that given to those who don't have by those who have; it may be money, strength, knowledge, bravery or hospitality.
46. Those who do not have divinity and humanity cannot follow virtue.

47. Life theories are of two types:

    1. Theory of God.

    2. Theory of karma.

48. The lives of those who belong to God depend on the theory of God. The life of those who do not have God depends on the theory of karma.

49. Experiencing the results by themselves based on their own qualifications and deeds is the theory of karma.

50. Experiencing results which are not based on their qualifications and deeds, but only by the grace of God is the theory of God.

51. Food, clothes, home, and romance are personal things. These are related to body and culture – these are changeable.

52. Love, truth, faith, righteousness, and virtue are related to the soul and divine path – these are not changeable.

53. Those who have God have both bodily and spiritual aspects. Those who do not have God have only bodily aspects.

54. Those who are related to God give value and importance to spiritual things than to bodily things.

55. Those who know God give more importance to spiritual things. Those who do not know God give more importance to bodily things.

56. Two types of humans:

    1. Those who know God.

    2. Those who don't know God.

57. Those who are away from God:

    1. They think highly of themselves.

    2. They will become corrupt.

    3. They will enjoy luxuries.

    4. They will become wicked.

    5. They will become cruel.

58. Those who have God:

    1. They will humble themselves.
    2. They will correct themselves.
    3. They will have happiness and be within limits.
    4. They will have order.
    5. They will have peace and freedom.

-2-

Prayers, Worship, Devotees, Way

59. Get to know God before you worship God.
60. The thing you must know about the God you are worshipping and adoring:

    1. He should be more sacred than you.

    2. He should be living.

    3. He should listen to your prayers.

    4. He should answer your prayers.
61. All those who worship God are not righteous, virtuous and holy people.

    Righteous are those who fear God.

    Virtuous are those who are liked by God.

    Holy are those who follow the truth.
62. Worship and prayers do not satisfy God, but satisfy you. Following orders of God gives satisfaction to God, you will get exertion, benison and blessing.
63. Prayer is not just related to words. Absolute prayer is the combination of heart, word and deed.
64. Only the prayer that is offered with soul and truth reaches God.
65. Those who want appreciation of people pray openly. Those who want appreciation of God pray in isolation.
66. Prayer is of two types:

    1. Prayer that asks.

    2. Prayer that listens.

67. This is how God's people must pray for their enemies:

    1. Praying that they must change their mind.

    2. Praying to avoid harm from them.

    3. Praying to be kept in a higher position than them.

68. Your true worship of God means following the orders of God, but not extolling God.

69. Worships of human beings are of two types:

    1. Worshiping with soul and truth based on God.

    2. Worshiping with body and mind based on self-interest.

70. Admiration and result will come from humans to the prayers and worship, which are done with the visible body, clothes, decorations and objects.

71. Admiration and result will come from God to the prayers and worship, which are done with no visible soul, love, truth or ethics.

72. Divinity is not something a person can achieve by himself, divinity is given by God to a person whom he loves.

73. One person does not belong to God just by worshipping God. Those who submit themselves totally to God will become devotees of God and belong to God.

74. Two types of devotees:

    1. Devotees that God seeks.

    2. Devotees that seek God.

75. God tries to control the devotees that God seeks. Devotees that seek God try to determine and control God.

76. A person can become a devotee of God, servant of God, man of God, and Son of God, but cannot become a God.

77. Impersonators cannot get a result from God.

78. Attire can get the appreciation of humans, but not God's appreciation.

79. To the deeds that seek the appreciation of visible humans cannot get the result from invisible God.
80. To the deeds that seek the appreciation of humans will get appreciation and result from humans. The deeds done by obeying God and the orders of God will get appreciation and result from God.
81. None of what a person gives to God can be accepted unless he submits his heart to God. In the eyes of God, there will not be value to what that person has given.
82. There is no value in the eyes of God for the prayers, offerings, sufferings and happiness of a person who has no conscience.
83. Reason why God's offerings are not giving results:

    1. Giving to get noticed by others.
    2. Giving with some expectations.
    3. Giving by grumble.
84. Your prayers and worship should be known to God, but not to the people.
85. Living as people of God or as the witness of God means:

    1. Following the path of God (path of truth).
    2. Having covenanted with God.
    3. Giving more value to God than themselves.
    4. Serving for the work of God.
    5. Being obedient to God.
    6. Dedicating the life to God.
    7. Admitting mistakes, sins and weaknesses before God.
    8. Removing things that God does not like in us.
    9. Leading a powerful and wonderful life.
86. Any path of God should be built on the roots of truth, virtue, justice, love, holiness and morals. Otherwise, it is not the path of God.

87. No religion is required for those who have and follow love, truth and honesty. Those who do not have these need a path of God, which has these and will teach these.

88. If you cannot follow, any scripture or any path of God is a waste for you.

89. All those who chose the path of God cannot walk in God's path. Only those who have the help of God can walk in the path of God.

90. If God is one, then the path is also one. If there are too many Gods, then there will be too many paths. It is better to search for one God in one path compared to searching for many Gods in many paths.

91. In the idols, the workmanship of the maker can be seen, but not God.

92. Humans can build temples and idols, but cannot create God.

93. Human being is more valuable than idols and temples. Because all these are made by humans.

94. Those who understand God say that God is in you, in the soul and in the whole creation, but did not say that God stays in only idols in temples.

-3-

Blessings

95. Purpose of blessing:

    1. Glory to God. 2. Glory to those who are blessed.
96. Blessing can't be received in a day. It can be received after winning many exertions with the help of God.
97. If someone does not have the blessing in him, there is a chance that a curse can enter him.
98. Blessings from God will remove the curse from a person's life and destroy the root cause of the curse.
99. Blessing without protection is dangerous.
100. Blessing is invisible; only the results of it are visible.
101. Blessings are related to the soul.
102. Blessing is ability.
103. One must be ready to work hard to reap the fruits of blessing.
104. When hard work is accompanied by blessing, the results will be better and superior.
105. A person who is responsible and trustable will be blessed.
106. Persons who refuse the blessing of God will become worthless.
107. Blessing comes from wisdom.

-4-

Religion, Spiritual, Conscience

108. Religion is that if a person worships God, many people also worship God like him.
109. Religion is a procedure of devotion set up by humans but not by God.
110. If a religion is established today, will another God be born? No religion was established by God.
111. If you really understand God, you won't follow any religious rites.
112. To pray to God, why do you choose the religion that was founded by someone else, long ago? Offer prayers in your own way.
113. Religions are the methods to people worship God. But there are no commands to worship God in the same manner as other.
114. Religion does not give salvation from sins. Salvation from sin can be achieved by having fear and faith in God.
115. If your mind thinks about religion, then you cannot understand God. If you understand God, you won't think about religion.
116. The people who related to religions have only words. The people who related to God have words and acts also.
117. Those who love God belong to God. Those who like religion belong to religion.
118. For all those who don't understand God, whatever they do in any religion is the same. All those who understand God, whatever they do in any religion is the same.
119. All superstitious believers are the same in any religion. There is no use for them to God and for their lives.

120. Religions are created by humans; that is why they are so many.
121. Some people get love from the path of God. Some people utilize religion to show hate within them.
122. Religion is a path to know God, but a few people give more value and focus on the path than on God. Thus, they don't know about God. Because of this, religion becomes bad in someone's view.
123. Path of God don't suggest hating human, but humans utilize religions to use hate within them.
124. God gave his words to different types of people in different ways and at different times, but humans created religion from these.
125. Religions are made by humans. That is why there may be faults in religions.
126. There are no commands that a person must follow a religion. And one can live without following any religion.
127. Religion without truth is superstition.
128. Holy books are the life paths set up by God. Religions are devotional practices are set up by humans.
129. God's words are written in different forms, due to different languages and different cultures of humans.
130. Those who follow bodily things are relatives of religion.
131. That which gives importance to bodily things becomes religion. That which gives importance to spiritual things becomes spirituality.
132. Spirituality is not that is imitated; it should be followed.
133. Conscience is greater than religion.
134. Religion shows the religious teacher and the past things. Conscience shows God and the future.
135. A person with a conscience is more valuable than a person with religion, and he will be liked by God.
136. A person without conscience has no truth and honesty.

-5-

Soul, Heart

137. You cannot see God with your eyes but can know God with your soul.
138. You can't hear the word of God with ears but can understand it with the soul.
139. God is the only one who can give a soul to you.
140. Soul, spiritual sayings are reflections of God. Those who have these belong to God.
141. There is no value in the view of God for the bodies that don't have a soul and chastity.
142. God has the authority to keep or remove the soul in your body.
143. Life will be in every living being. But everyone cannot have a soul.
144. You should not live your life as per other people's determination; you should live as per your soul. Your Soul is superior to the world.
145. If you feel that want to spend time with yourself, it means you have recognized your soul.
146. Peace and answers are related to the soul.
147. Soul and spiritual sentences are required to understand God.
148. God connects with you through soul and prophecies.
149. A believer is a combination of a soul and a body.
150. There are two types of human beings:

    1. Those who follow the soul.

    2. Those who follow the body.
151. Your soul can guide your body but your body cannot guide your soul.

152. A human can understand God in two ways:

 1. Through soul.

 2. Through the words of God.

153. Two types of knowledge about God:

 1. Human knowledge about God. There may or may not have faults and suspicion in this manner.

 2. God, letting the human know about him. There will be no faults and suspicion in the manner.

154. The strength of the soul is stronger than any other strength.

155. We can please only humans with bodily aspects, but not God.

156. We cannot please all humans with spiritual aspects, but we can please God.

157. Those who follow spiritual aspects belong to God.

158. It's a big sin to kill those who have a soul.

159. Rebirths are for souls, but not for bodies and humans.

160. Mediator between God and humans – soul.

161. If someone kills a person who has a soul, that person and his generation will be cursed.

162. If someone is meditating on spiritual and moral sentences that means that they are gaining spiritual strength.

163. The deeds of the soul:

 1. Causing discretion of what is good and what is bad.

 2. Making them admit blunders, mistakes and sins done in the past.

 3. Giving strength to prevent wickedness and committing sins.

 4. Being a bridge between God and humans and leading to the proximity of God.

 5. To help being truthful, holy and righteous.

6. Communicating thoughts, words and deeds of God.

7. Teaching and leading the duty of life.

164. Those who do not have a soul do not have the discernment, mental capacity, wisdom, love, holiness, involvement of God and duty management abilities.

165. Truth, love, conscience, faith, morality, wisdom, bravery, happiness and compassion for the soul are like organs to the body.

166. The soul is needed to get the mercy of God.

167. The soul can travel faster than time.

168. The holy spirit is not something that everyone can get. This is given by God to those who he chooses.

169. Those who get the holy spirit are born for a purpose.

170. Soul, Holy Spirit and God are not the same.

171. Even when a soul is not present in a body, it can function with the senses.

172. You will get faith because of your soul. You will get a soul from God.

173. Food for the soul:

1. Spiritual statements.

2. Moral statements.

174. Getting to heaven means that change your mind and being born again spiritually.

175. Hygiene and cleanliness are related to the body and surroundings. Sanctity and purity are related to the soul (heart).

176. Renaissance happens to humans. Rebirth happens to the soul.

177. People who don't have self-respect cannot get delighted and have peace of mind.

178. Things that you cannot do with your power, strength, money and education, can be done with the soul given by God.

179. Spiritual things are those that decide whether God is present in your life or not, but not your bodily things.
180. Souls have memories, circumspection and goal.
181. Conscience to the soul is like the eye to the body.
182. The same person cannot worship both idol and the soul.
183. God, soul and spiritual statements can transform wicked

And sinners into the finest persons.
184. One cannot become a righteous and holy person through bodily functions but can become one by soul.
185. Those who do not have a soul cannot believe in God and his deeds.
186. Those who separate souls and live with the body are hypocrites.
187. The two types of humans:

1. Those who belong to the evil soul.

2. Those who belong to God.
188. Those who related to an evil soul like and support to harm others.
189. Those who related to God like and support only to help others.
190. You won't become a devotee by visiting temples but you can when you surrender your heart to God and get the grace of God.
191. God looks at your heart when you sleep.
192. People will look at your body and deeds.

God observes your heart and thoughts.
193. You cannot know God with your tough and unforgiving heart.
194. Earn your soul; it will earn everything for you.
195. If a body is functioning with sense organs, he is a normal man. If a body is functioning with a soul, he is a believer in God. If a body is functioning with Holy Spirit, he is an uncommon man, a man of God.

-6-

Apologies, Repentance, Life

196. If you admit your wrongs and sins honestly, God will be ever ready to forgive you and give new life to you.
197. No matter how many wrongs and sins you have committed, God will forgive you as long as you don't repeat and seek forgiveness; God also gives power not to repeat the mistake.
198. If you cannot seek forgiveness from those whom you have harmed, then ask God for forgiveness.
199. If God forgives you, then it will be enough.
200. If you forgive others, God will forgive you.
201. God forgives you in those matters in which you forgive others.
202. Those who have no mercy get the judgment that has no mercy.
203. Those who forgive receive forgiveness.
204. Those who receive forgiveness are not eligible for punishment.
205. All those who are clean are not chaste. All those who are unclean are not impure.
206. Possessing cleanliness and hygiene does not mean having holiness and purity.
207. Cleanliness without hygiene has no value.
208. A person changing as a holy man begins by admitting his mistakes and sins.
209. Those who commit mistakes, wrongs and sins are eligible for forgiveness. Those who are involved in cheating betrayal and conspiracy are eligible for punishment.

210. If you are remembering the mistakes, sins and worst things you have committed, then what you should do is– ask for forgiveness from God.

211. If you are still not punished, it means that you are still eligible for forgiveness. But it does not mean that God does not know about your wrongs, sins and betrayals.

212. The reason why the result of wrongs and sins committed by a person remains and suffers because of not getting forgiveness.

213. Those who can forgive any wrongs, sins and anyone at any time in any situation is God

214. If you accept your wrongs, you get forgiveness; it helps you not to repeat the wrongs.

215. No one in the world that don't make wrongs. People who repent and do not repeat the same wrongs are righteous people.

216. If you are justifying your wrongs, it means that you are trying to repeat the wrong.

217. If you repent for the wrongs you have done, then you are blessed.

218. Man's prayers that God likes most are:

    1. Prayer for repentance.

    2. Praying with repentance.

219. To change your mind, you only need to repent for the wrongs you have done, but to change your life you need the help of God.

220. God forgives these people:

    1. Those who are repenting for the wrongs and sins they have done.

    2. Those who are trying not to repeat their wrongs and sins.

    3. Those who accept their weaknesses.

    4. Those who are trying to correct themselves.

221. God punishes these people:

    1. Those who are trying to harm others repeatedly.

2. Those who are not changing even if an opportunity is given.

3. Those who do not change within the time given to change.

222. If mistakes are more – wrong.

If wrongs are more – sin.

If sins are more – death.

223. More negligence is equal to sin.

224. If a mistake happens without your knowledge and will, then it is the responsibility of the situation but not yours.

225. The blunders, mistakes and sins you commit are of two types:

1. Those others can bear.

2. Those you only should bear and suffer.

226. You have to forgive the enemy, who asks for forgiveness, but not the opponent or enemy who is destroying you.

227. If you underestimate a person and cheat him repeatedly, you will lose forgiveness.

228. You have the right to point out others' wrongs only if you do not commit any wrongs.

229. If you accept it will become blunders, mistakes and sins. If you keep covering and justifying, it will become cheating, betrayal and fraud.

230. If you keep on forgiving a person repeatedly, then you are responsible for the wrong he is going to commit later.

The more you can forgive people and wrongs, the stronger you are. The more you cannot forgive people and wrongs, the more you are weaker.

231. You can forgive and trust those who accept their wrongs, but you should not forgive and trust those who cover their wrongs.

232. You will get independence and strength by asking for forgiveness for your mistakes.

233. If you admit a wrong, it becomes a mistake. If you cover a wrong it becomes betrayal.

234. Forgive and help some people. Forgive and leave some people.

235. Mental weakness that doesn't allow asking for forgiveness and that don't forgive others will be the cause of losing a relationship.

-7-

Believer, Faith, Trust

236. Trustworthy are:

    1. God. 2. Those who believe in God.

237. Nothing is impossible for these two:

    1. God. 2. Those who believe in God.

238. Believers are lights lit by God.

239. Believers can do everything, but they don't do anything which is not safe and which are not liked by God without any reason or need.

240. Those who focus only on visible things cannot be believers.

241. Infidelity is the obstruction to the goal of a believer.

242. The word that there is the existence of God belongs to faith. The word that there is no God belongs to trust.

243. You will get trust because of your sense organs. You get faith because of your soul.

244. Trust occurs when you have a source. Faith occurs when there is no source.

245. You not only have to believe in God, but you also have to believe in what God gave you.

246. Those who have faith in God can never be ashamed.

247. You need to have faith in God or you need to believe in yourself. Otherwise, you cannot achieve anything.

248. You may or may not become successful if you believe in this world and human beings. But you can be successful if you believe in God.

249. Those who keep their faith in God will get peace.

250. You can keep complete faith in God alone.

251. The relationship between two persons who have faith in God is greater than the relationship between two people who trust each other.

252. Expectation from God - trustworthy. The expectation from humans - unbelievable.

253. Trust will emanate from everyone. Faith will emanate from only a few people who have a soul.

254. Faith will not be to those who have no soul.

255. There is someone that you can have faith in than anything or anyone – God.

-8-

Morality, Honesty, Fact

256. Morality lets you know what is good and what is bad by following the truth based on time and situations.
257. Being fact means feeling that God knows what you are thinking, talking and doing.
258. Those who want protection and involvement of God in their lives must live with honesty and fact.
259. If you are meditating on spiritual statements and moral sentences, it means you are trying to get the strength of the soul.
260. Those who live righteously and in reality become the people of God.
261. This world observes your body, money, education and race. God observes your heart, honesty, realization and thoughts.
262. Whatever race, religion or country you belong to, God blesses you as much as you live with reality and honesty.
263. Everyone likes God, but God likes factual and honest people and provides them with His divine qualities.

-9-

Chastity, Holy, Sin

264. Chastity means purity of heart.
265. You have beauty and attraction until you have personality.
266. Holiness is the root of divine thoughts, words and deeds.
267. When thought, word and deed are the same, it is holiness.
268. The measure of holiness is purity.
269. Being clean is a good thing. Being holy is a great thing.
270. A person who follows the truth can never become unholy.
271. Truth can never become unholy.
272. Those who do not have a soul can never become holy people.
273. Holiness is not related to the body. It is related to the heart.
274. Holiness does not depend on good or bad.
275. Holiness is beyond good and bad.
276. If you can live with holiness, nature befriends you.
277. When a sin is committed, it feels good for a short time, but in the long time, it will lead to diseases and suffering.
278. When you're getting holiness, things will be bitter for a short time, but there will be delight and health permanently.
279. Holiness causes faith and courage. Sin causes cowardice and fear.
280. Holiness causes strength and success. Sin causes weakness and defeat.
281. To get rid of sin within you, there should be no sin in your thoughts, words and deeds. That's when sin is gone from you.

282. Your sin and holiness are determined by your thoughts, words and deeds.

283. If wrong things happen once without knowing it is a mistake. If wrong happens once with knowing it is wrong. If wrong happens repeatedly with knowing, it is sin.

284. If you suffer due to the sins of your elders, it is foolishness. Getting forgiveness and mercy by knowing God is wisdom.

285. Liking sin and committing sin are two different things.

286. Those who like sins might not commit them or are not able to do them. Those who don't like sins may commit or be able to commit them. Sin is not present in the work we do; it will be there in the way we do it.

287. Sinners are of two types:

1. Those who do it by self.

2. Those who do along with others.

288. Sins committed individually:

Cheating yourself; cheating your soul.

Giving more value to things that obstruct your goals, aims and responsibilities.

Ignoring your goals, aims and responsibilities even when you have the ability.

Becoming a slave to things that you feel are wrong.

289. Sins done with others:

Giving unjust judgment, false evidence, repeatedly committing mistakes, acting corruptly, unjustly, unrighteous and illegally, justifying the mistakes, harming those who had done good, being greedy, killing, cheating the self and others for self-interest, having no compassion for others, to demean others, doing deeds differently from your words, cheating society, and creating wrong words, wrong paths and wrong theories against moral values and teaching them. To deceive, enslave, backbite and conspire for self-interest.

290. Sin spreads in different forms in different places. That is why God incarnate is in different forms in different places.

291. It will be a sin when doing uncontrollable things either physically or mentally.

292. Those who want to live happily without struggling commit sins. Living with honesty and fact will be a cause to gain holiness.

-10-

Power, Tasks, Policy, Relation, Help

293. God is not a power; God is the creator and controller of powers.
294. Powers are there for you to use, but not for appearing to you.
295. Divine deeds cannot be done through human power.
296. A human tries to control things that appear to him. That is why, to control humans, God created powers that do not appear.
297. Human beings cannot determine divine deeds.
298. Only God can decide the eligibility of human beings perform divine deeds. But not human beings.
299. The eligibility of people to do divine deeds should be determined by God and not by human beings.
300. Deeds done without the will of God do not get fruits from God.
301. Thoughts and deeds of God are beyond the thoughts and deeds of human beings.
302. When people need justice, deeds have to happen. For deeds to happen, a path should be created. A leader must be born to create a path. The decision of God should happen for the leader to be born. For the decision of God to happen, people must go to God and pray to him.
303. God does not need those who praise God, God needs those who need God and who do the deeds of God.
304. Implications, hardships, troubles, insults and accidents will be there in the deeds of God.
305. Those who are born for God, who gained Godliness, and who work for God are called Goddesses, messengers of God and servants of God.

306. God may or may not visit a person or another person in the same manner.

307. The following situations should present for God to help:

1. When human beings cannot do any help. Or

2. When there are no human beings to help.

308. The help of God does not come early or late. It comes at the right time.

309. Ways to get the help of God:

1. Soul. 2. Spiritual statements. 3. Love.

310. God helps a man through his soul. Man gets the help of God through spirituality. Man gets help from the love of other men. Those who want to depend on others cannot get help from God.

311. There is no great saviour than God.

312. Protection of God is permanent. The protection of a human being is temporary.

313. Goddesses, powers and humans and things will be in the process of God's protection. Humans and things will be in the process of human protection.

314. In the matters of determining a person, the way of God and the way of humans are different.

315. The ways in which God own a person:

1. Letting him be re-born with a soul.

2. Getting God's presence to accompany him.

3. Letting him know of God's thoughts.

4. Not leaving him based on his mistakes.

5. Giving the mercy of God to him.

316. No one can test a person in the way God tests.

317. If God tests a man, more good happens to him than harm. If a man tests God, more harm happens to him than good.

318. God looks at both good and bad people.

319. Human beings cannot change the decisions of God. God can change the decisions of human beings.

320. There are matters created by God. There are matters also made by God.

321. Human beings make matters and things. God creates matters and things.

322. Human beings cannot create the matters and things that God created. But human beings can change matters and things that human beings made.

323. Body, money, food, trust, intelligence, and education – belong to human beings. Wisdom, faith, soul, love, hunger, and sleep – belong to God.

324. No one can offer service to God without being useful to human beings.

325. God does not harm everyone who commits mistakes because God loves everyone. But God will definitely do harm to those who harm those who are set up by God.

326. The more harm is done to the people who belong to God, the more harm happens to those who harm the people of God.

327. Those who do good to those who are set up by God will get good. Those who do harm to those who are set up by God will get harmed. Those who have enmity toward those who are set up by God will become enemies of God. Those who have antagonism to those who are set up by God will become antagonistic to God.

328. Those who are Gods give a person:

     Body, love, wisdom, faith, intelligence, power, beauty, health, education, skill, status and glory. Based on the life he has to lead, God may or may not give all these to a person at the same time.

329. God does not give what you want, at the time you want, in the way you want. God gives what he wants to give, at what time he wants to give and in the way he wants to give.

330. God works strongly on these people:

    1. On those whom he loves.

    2. On those who harm the people he loves.

    3. On those who feel that they are greater than God.

331. The reasons why God does not give to you or remove something from you:

    1. Because those do not bring good for you.

    2. Because there are chances that they will harm you.

    3. They will be obstructing your development.

    4. There is a chance to get things better than those.

332. The one who can see the past, present and future of a person, and let the person know about them – God.

333. God will help some people sometimes who make war, but God will not help anyone at any time to those who harm others.

334. God is holy. Thus, he wants others to be holy. God is powerful; thus, he can punish, forgive or do good.

335. Those who have God in their hearts can understand God.

336. Whatever God begins, it gets completed.

-11-

Heaven, Hell

337. Heaven is not somewhere after the body is dead. Life is heaven that continues by following the soul and understanding God.

338. If you have divinity in your heart, you are in heaven. If you have evil in your heart, you are in hell.

339. God curses and gives hell to those who justify and cover their wrongs. God loves, punishes and gives heaven to those who try not to repeat the wrongs. These do not happen after death; these happen on the earth while you're still alive.

340. Living in the light of truth is heaven.

341. Qualities and attributes of those who experience the life of heaven: love, peace, kindness, mercy, gentleness, truth, modesty, good words, helping, zeal, answer, freedom, independence, honesty and courage.

342. Qualities and attributes of those who experience a life of hell: hatred, abuse, arrogance, pride, lust, addictions, attire, pretend, overeating, over drinking, oversleeping, untruth, jealousy, envy, cheating, betrayal, slavery, mental weakness and cowardice.

-12-

Life

343. If you know about God, you can know about yourself and your life.

344. When you want the involvement of God in your life, you must be ready to lose what God does not like in you.

345. Whatever the aspects you assign to God, there will be involvement of God in only those aspects.

346. There will be some things in your life that will be done by God. There will be some things that God makes through you.

347. The reasons why there is happiness in your life:

    1. Because God is there in your life.

    2. Because you have a goal.

    3. Because you are honest.

348. The one who can correct your life and dreams which are shattered – God.

349. Everybody's life is not predetermined or pre-written. It is created depending on the parents, persons and situations around them and their ability.

350. Everybody's life will not be predetermined. The life and responsibilities of those who are chosen by God are predetermined.

351. Those who cannot continue their lives can continue with the help of God. They can depend on God. From then, their life is decided by God.

352. God is interested in those who have an aversion towards their life.

353. Life's belonging to God are:

1. Lives that depend on God.

2. Lives that are handed over to God.

354. Future and development will be for the deeds, lives and human beings which are assigned to God.

355. God is present only in the lives of those who live by obeying God's decisions. God will not be present in the lives of those who pray to God in favour of their decisions.

356. Everyone has the need for God, but God is not present in everyone's life.

357. God's glory in any person's life depends on the good that happens in his life.

358. Life that understands God will be like climbing a hill.

359. Life after understanding God will be like walking down a hill.

-13-

Love

360. Love is a divine quality; it is the prime quality of God.
361. All the paths of God are for you to remember the humanity in you and to fill love in your heart.
362. Loving God is to follow his orders because he observes you every day, every time.
363. All are equal to God. The more you love God, the more God loves you.
364. Please remember, no one can love you more than God.
365. First, get the love of God, and then, share their love with them.
366. When you have everything, everyone will like you and want you. When you do not have anything, God and the people of God only love you and want you.
367. Whatever the way of God is useless to the person when you cannot give love to him.
368. What lets you live even if the relationships like mother, father, girlfriend, boyfriend, brother, younger brother, elder and younger sisters, friends and relations are not there is – the love of God.
369. Blessed are those who get the love of God; they do not lose happiness, even if they have no relations with human beings.
370. God can love anyone.

-14-

Strength, Weakness

371. God lays the path and gives you strength and power to walk, but walking is yours.

372. How much ever you depend on God in your weakness, God gives you that much strength.

373. When people in this world hate you, know that God who is stronger than them loves you.

374. In the eyes of the world:

     The person who has money – strong man.

     The person who does not have money – waste and weak.

     In the eyes of God:

     The person who has money is rich.

     The person who has love – strong and powerful.

-15-

Fear, Dare

375. Have the fear of God, and then, you need not fear anyone.
376. Blessed are those who take shelter from God.
377. The fear that never goes once it emanates is the fear of God.
378. You can do nothing if you fear the world.
379. You can do anything if you fear God.
380. When you feel fear, there should be something that gives you courage. No one can give you more courage than God.
381. The courage one gets from God is great and more useful than the courage one gets from birth, money and power.
382. Fear of behaviour and fear of God is better than fear of human beings.
383. Those who fear human beings cannot become righteous. Those who fear their behaviour and God become righteous.
384. Those who do not have fear of God are not considered human beings.
385. Fear and bravery emanate because God never leaves you.
386. Those who fear God do not fear anything.
387. Many things will obey those who obey God.
388. Those who fear God:

    1. Will live by submitting to God.
    2. Will admits their mistakes.
    3. Will hate badness.
    4. Will like to do good.

-16-

Money, Needs

389. Love, faith, and wisdom are the most valuable things that God gives you. If you really understand God, you will get these things from God.

390. If you do not understand God, you will ask for money, education, ornaments and vehicles from God.

391. Reasons why you are poor:

    1. Believing human beings.

    2. Because God didn't give you.

392. Selfless help is a loan given to God.

393. You know better what you want; God knows even better than you.

394. There may be faults in what you ask God, but there won't be any faults in what God gives you.

395. God knows better what, how and where to give you.

396. Before giving you what you need, God removes what you do not need. Do not feel bad about it.

397. Know what God had given him by looking at great people. Know what God gave you by looking into yourself or through God.

398. When God wants to give you, he will not let others give you.

399. A person's life is influenced by the invisible life, love, wisdom, sleep and hunger than the visible body, money, clothes and food.

400. God is not needed for food, money, education, intelligence, clothes and ornaments. Man can also earn these.

401. Even people wish to get faithfulness, love, life, wisdom, delight and health, but they won't get them without God.

-17-

Exertion, Difficulty

402. Exertion is God's attribute.
403. God loves exertion.
404. There will be exertions in the deeds done for God, people and others.
405. You will be the favourite of God if you bear the sufferings and exertions involved when doing good to others.
406. When there is nobody with you in your suffering and needs, then God will be there with you.
407. The meaning of the suffering you are getting is that God is teaching you something. You will understand this after the suffering is over.

-18-

Profession, Work

408. Your profession is the work provided to you by God. Working honestly is also a part of prayer.
409. Your profession is the skill that God gave to you.

-19-

Commands, Words

410. Following the orders of God will bring good to you but not to God.

411. Blessing by following the orders of God:

    1. Everything in our life becomes good.
    2. Your prayers reach God.
    3. All your wishes will be fulfilled.
    4. Your offerings are accepted.
    5. You will know what to ask.
    6. You will get security.
    7. You will get wisdom.
    8. You will get leadership.
    9. You will not have dearth.
    10. You can know the mystery of God.

412. The words a person can hear:

    1. Words of God.
    2. Words of human beings.
    3. Words of the world.
    4. Words of scoundrel people.

413. To trust the words of God one must have faith. To get faith, one must listen to the words of God.

414. Words of God:

    1. Will be beyond the knowledge of the world.
    2. Will be the roots of faith.

415. The words of God:

1. Will be the truth. 2. Will have life. 3. Will provide wisdom. 4. Will provoke thoughts. 5. Will provide strength and power. 6. Will Influence.

416. God's words are such that they are unbelievable to humans. Words of humans are such that they are believed by human beings. The words of the world are similar to what happens in the world. The words of scoundrel people are untrue.

417. The words of God will connect to these people:

1. Those who search for God.

2. Those who seek wisdom.

3. Those whose heart is broken and crumpled.

4. Those who are in a poor condition.

5. Those who lost the upholding of human beings.

418. The people who are valued in the view of God:

1. They will have fear of God.

2. They will have faith in God.

3. They will have a conscience.

419. God likes those:

1. Who are righteous and realistic.

2. Who have faith in God.

3. Who have a broken or crushed heart.

420. God hates those:

1. Who are disobedient to the truth.

2. Who cheat themselves.

3. Who create differences between people.

4. Who have jealousy and envy.

-20-

Creation

421. God created nature for man. All creatures except man are part of nature.

422. Nature that keeps people alive, succumbs to God, but human beings will not succumb to God.

423. Things that are impossible for you:

    1. Going to a place where there is no God.

    2. Doing something without the knowledge of God.

    3. Thinking something without letting God know.

424. A child has only one father – one creation has only one God.

425. Humans cannot know the origin and end of creation. Because God has created the creation, not a human being.

-21-

You, To You, For You, In You

426. Everything which cannot be done with your power and strength in your life is done by God.
427. There will be situations in which you can understand your plans. There will be some situations in which you cannot understand the plans of God.
428. Don't you have anyone? Then, God is there for you.
429. Depend on those who are below you and poor if you want to give anything.
430. If you want something, depend on your superiors and God.
431. You will get glory and majesty because of God.
432. Whatever God gives you, you have to use it as per the will of God.
433. God tells you his ideas through his soul, statements, songs and prophecies.
434. God can tell you his thoughts, give something to you, or get something done by you only when you completely surrender to God.
435. When you are alone, God tries to tell you his thoughts.
436. You must visit temples to know and understand God.
437. First, understand God; then ask for a boon.
438. Boon without fruit is useless.
439. God knows what, where, how you are doing and what you are thinking. God watches you too.
440. You may not learn anything, but God can teach you everything.
441. If you are obedient to God, you will know what freedom is.

442. Do not feel proud about what you achieve, God arranged for you to be a servant to achieve it.

443. You can cheat yourself and you can cheat others but you cannot cheat God in any way.

444. In some situations, neither you nor your parents cannot control you, but God can control you.

445. You get innovation if you have creativity in you. You will get creativity from God.

-22-

Other Sentences

446. The greatest relationship of all – is the relationship between God and man.
447. How can he become a God if humans can fully understand God? What difference is there between God and humans? Thus, those who don't understand God will say that God doesn't exist, and others say this is God. Whatever they understand as God.
448. Goddesses are known to everyone but God is not known to all.
449. God is not present in every person; God is present in persons where there is opportunity.
450. Those who consider themselves greater than God do not belong to God.
451. Upholding God is greater than upholding human beings.
452. People who don't have a father and a husband, and who are orphans and poor are representatives of God on earth. How you behave with them is what reaches God.
453. God is not a human being to appear to everyone.
454. Determining God is what can never be done by human beings.
455. The people who have a relationship with God will have divine qualities.
456. A righteous wife is a blessing to her husband.
457. A righteous husband is a blessing to his wife.
458. Blessed are those who are kind towards the poor; they will get the kindness of God.

459. Blessed are those who show mercy on the poor. They will get mercy from God.

460. Food is created by human beings for hunger, which is created by God.

461. God likes gratitude.

462. Birth and death are for human beings, living things who are created by God, not for God.

463. If a person is determining God, it means he is trying to be in a higher status than God.

464. Nobody can value those who have value in the eyes of God.

465. The people who have pride are those who do not know completely about God.

466. Human beings cannot define God, soul and creation.

467. Those who harm others will become God's enemies; they will get the fruit of evil.

468. People who turn away from God are going close to apostasy.

469. Those who turn away from God become enemies to the people of God.

470. The world will know about those who know about God.

471. All those who talk about God don't know God.

472. People who do good to those who harm them – people of God.

People who do good to those who do good to them – human beings.

People who harm those who did good to them – wicked.

473. The most powerful than everyone and everything, and the greatest one – God.

PART TWO

PERSON

-1-

Truth, Love, Faith, Wisdom, Intelligence

474. Truth, love, faith, wisdom, honesty, fact, justice and virtue is the sequence of priority matters in your life.

475. Truth, love, belief, and knowledge are stronger and more powerful than ethnicity, caste, religion, power, education, intelligence and money.

476. If you have love, faith, and wisdom in yourself, region, religion, caste, money, education, power and others cannot give you respect and disrespect.

477. Love, friendship, honesty, wisdom and truth are valuable and sacred; do not expect these from everyone.

478. If you follow the truth, you can become an independent, sacred and honest person.

479. If you don't accept the truth, there will be no delight and development in you.

480. Science and truth are different.

     Experience and truth are different.

     Opinion and truth are different.

481. If you walk in the path of truth, bravery follows you and leads you forward.

482. No qualification is needed to know truth, and wisdom and to be loved.

483. You need to know the truth yourself at some point.

484. Whatever you earn with truthfulness protects you. You need to protect the things that you earn with falsehood.

485. You have to pretend to get the things that you earn by pretending.

486. Education, however, is great, but useless if it doesn't teach you courteousness, knowledge and discipline.

487. Education makes you a good person. Wisdom makes you a great person.

488. Earn wisdom; it will earn whatever you want.

489. The more knowledge you gain, the more strength you will get. The more intelligence you have to use for wisdom, the more powerful you will become.

490. Wisdom is light for your path. This shows the path to your goal.

491. Your wisdom is the light for your life.

492. You have to earn wisdom to understand the matters of the world. But do not understand matters in the world with your intelligence.

493. Wisdom is greater than knowledge.

494. Wisdom means knowing yourself and knowing for yourself. Knowledge is you knowing about the world.

495. Wisdom causes happiness and delight. Ignorance causes pain and agony.

496. The reason for your non-development is not only because of other people; it is your ignorance too.

497. Physical laziness leads to poor health and non-development. Mental sluggishness causes a lack of mental thinking and lack of knowledge.

498. If you see something useless, it means you have no wisdom to use it. There is no useless thing in this creation.

499. More dangerous than illiteracy is ignorance.

500. If questioned for wisdom, you will get wisdom. If questioned with wisdom, wisdom will emanate.

501. Types of questioning:
   1. Questioning with ignorance.
   2. Questioning for wisdom.
   3. Questioning with wisdom.

502. Types of questioning with ignorance:
   1. Questioning even after knowing.
   2. Questioning to trouble.
   3. Questioning to get a favourable answer.

503. Ignorance in you hurts others.

504. Intelligence escapes the problem. Wisdom eliminates the problem.

505. Knowing and understanding are different things. Intelligence is needed to know. Wisdom is required to understand.

506. Intelligence is temporary. Wisdom – is permanent.

507. Intelligence is of two types:
   1. Intelligence with wisdom.
   2. Intelligence with ignorance.

508. The more you underestimate the intelligence of another person, the more your intelligence is diminished in you.

509. Having intelligence in you is not a big matter; animals, birds and insects also possess this.

510. If a person is not filled with truth, righteousness, wisdom and faith, untruth, corruption, ignorance and weakness will occupy him.

-2-

Soul, Heart, Mind, Body

511. Spiritually – soul. Socially – we call it heart.

512. Good food is required to keep your body healthy.

513. Good spirituality is required to keep your heart healthy.

514. If you talk to a person with your mouth, it reaches his ear. If you talk to a person with a heart, it reaches his heart.

515. Your character is known by your words. Your heart is known through your behaviour.

516. You will be made by your heart. You will get by your behaviour.

517. Books give strength to your heart.

518. The greater the books you read, the stronger your heart will become.

519. When your heart is as clean as a mirror, the character of the opposite person appears clearly.

520. You should never make decisions according to the situation; rather, make decisions according to what your heart feels is the truth.

521. Consolation is the medication for heart injury.

522. Loneliness is of two types:

    1. Loneliness of the body.

    2. Loneliness of the heart.

523. Food, sleep and comfort, which are needed by the body should be within limits. There should not be limits to the love, friendship, freedom, and delight needed for the heart.

524. Your heart should not depend on your ethnicity, caste, religion, place, money and education; it should depend on your self-respect.

525. The body needs work; the heart needs a sport, art or service.

526. Your body enjoys visible things. Your heart enjoys invisible things.

527. Give freedom to the hearts of children, not to their bodies.

528. Whatever cultures and traditions your body is in, your heart must have humanity.

529. Character is not based on the mind; it is based on the heart.

530. Those who do not have a heart cannot have a personality.

531. Patience relates to the body; forbearance is related to the heart.

532. The chastity of men and women is not lost due to marriage or becoming prostitutes. It's lost due to betrayal and illicit thoughts and acts.

533. Chastity does not belong to the body; it belongs to the heart.

534. Chastity is the purity of heart.

535. Everyone has a mind. Only a few have a heart.

536. Your mind wants everything. Your heart wants only the things you need.

537. Your mind thinks about all necessary, unnecessary, good and bad things. Your heart takes and follows only what you want.

538. Everyone has a mind, only people who have personalities have a heart.

539. No matter how many bad thoughts come to your mind, they should not reach your heart.

540. Your mind should get angry but not your heart.

541. Your physical addictions may or may not spoil your body, but your mental addictions will definitely spoil your life.

542. Overeating, overdrinking, oversleeping, over comfort are physical addictions.

543. Prostitution is of two types:

    1. Mental prostitution. 2. Physical prostitution.

544. Physical prostitutes may not involve in mental prostitution.

545. Mental prostitutes may not involve in physical prostitution.

546. Physical prostitution: A body belongs to more than one person.

547. Mental prostitution:

1. Losing self-respect for needs.

2. Praising and insulting the same thing.

3. Having a difference between thoughts and words.

548. Two types of pretend:

1. Physical pretend. 2. Mental pretend.

549. Physical pretend:

1. Visible decoration on the body.

2. Body behaviour.

550. Mental pretend:

1. Having differences in thoughts and words.

2. Making an effort to be known as good, without being good.

551. To understand others, one should understand the situations of others. Mental ability is needed to understand the situations of others. Mental health is needed to have mental ability.

552. To be psychologically healthy, one should not have diseases and mental addictions.

553. Mentally weak persons cannot understand others.

554. Reasons for mental weakness:

1. Mental disabilities.

2. Mental diseases.

3. Mental addictions.

555. Mental disabilities:

1. Thought to depend on others.

2. Not having patience.

3. Laziness and cowardice.

4. Stupidity and slavery.

556. Mental diseases:

1. Hatred, jealousy, acting, selfishness.

2. Corruption, over-ambitiousness, greediness, partiality.

3. Cheating themselves and others.

4. Telling lies, betraying, deceiving.

557. Mental addictions:

1. Ethnicity, caste, religion, racial and regional differences.

2. Rich and poor differences, factions' differences.

558. Things that give mental strength:

1. Forbearance, determination, discipline.

2. Thinking, intelligence, and skill.

3. Impartiality, bravery, reality.

4. Truth, trust, gratitude.

5. Happiness, forgiveness, kindness.

559. Things which give strength to the soul:

Truth, love, wisdom, ethics, faith and compassion.

-3-

Life

560. You should definitely know why you are living.

561. If you want your life to appear beautiful and happy to yourself, you should do the thing that you like, or need to do things honestly.

562. If you want to like your life, you should like yourself.

563. If you want your life to be always new, you should keep learning something new.

564. If your life is not led forward by bravery, cowardice leads your life backwards.

565. Happiness in your life begins when you realize the fact that you will die sometime.

566. If you don't feel like dying even at least once in your lifetime; it is not at all life.

567. Your life is not only for you but also for those who believe in you and who depend on you.

568. Whatever good or bad happens in your life, it is not just for you.

569. The duty of your life is to lead a life without causing harm to other creatures.

570. The two words that are apt for your life:

    1. Don't do the work that needs to lie.

    2. Don't do something knowing that it is wrong.

571. Your way of things should be great. Your way of living should be simple.

572. Until you cheat yourself, you keep on losing yourself and your life.

573. If you cheat yourself, your life will also cheat you.

574. If you have the characteristic of cheating, it leads to losing yourself.

575. Cheating yourself does not make others get cheated.

576. If you are the person who cheat yourself, then you are the enemy of your own life, and you will be a burden to your people.

577. It is you, not the other who loses if you keep cheating yourself.

578. If you want to live freely like a human being, don't be like a person who belongs to a particular ethnicity, caste, religion or place.

579. Eat to live and do what you have to do, but do not live to eat.

580. Your greatness is not based on how good you live but is based on the good things that you have done for others.

581. To whom and where you will be born is not in your hands, but how you want to lead life is in your hands.

582. Your life must be built on values, not on standards.

583. Your life is more valuable than your aim.

584. If there is no honesty in what you do, there will be no development in your life.

585. The way torn clothes show your body is the way superstitious rituals show your life.

586. If you could identify your soul, it gives your life to you.

587. If your life is not useful to you, use it for others. There is no life that is not useful to others.

588. Since you live only once, it should be in the way you like. If not, you should change it.

589. Purity of heart is not giving place to bad thoughts. Leading a good life is not giving a place to things or persons that harm you.

590. You should live not by feeling it, but by following and experiencing it.

591. If you've lost everything in your life, it means you have gained something valuable, which can be spiritual, mental or personal.

592. Your life does not change by itself; you should change your life by yourself.

593. Your life is like a sculpture you are carving. It shows how much you changed it. But it does not change by itself.

594. Do not think about when your life will change, think about what to do to change your life and follow it.

595. Your life will be the same as your thoughts and deeds when you are alone.

596. The hardships you face due to your laziness make you lose your life. The hardships you face due to exertions make you grow in your life.

597. No other human being is able to stop your growth and development. Only your cowardice, laziness, lethargy, and the characteristic of cheating yourself can stop them.

598. Life is not about only making yourself or others happy; it's about making both yourself and others happy.

599. If any man creates anything against your life, you change it. Because you are also human.

600. In your life, you will face a few people who are there to love or hate you, help or get helped, teach or learn and support or cheat. Do not expect everything from everyone.

601. Your life is influenced by what you fear.

602. If you grow plants, it gives you fruits. If your parents raise you, you have to look after them. Your life should be like a plant that gives fruits.

603. Your life is led by what you give the most value.

604. If you live for a hundred years, it means you lived a full life. If you live like a human being, it means you lived a thorough life.

605. You must live your life by believing your mother's words in child age, your father's words in the growing stage, prophet's words at a young age and believe in yourself in middle age.

606. If you cheat God, your parents, yourself or others who give you life, you will not have life.

607. Having happiness and comfort does not mean that you have a life and future.

608. If you live with morals, you will love yourself.

609. The more you live with honesty, the more you will like yourself.

-4-

Ens, Philosophy, Personality, Habits, Attributes, Symptoms

610. Philosophy is that which is understood, learned and used.

611. Your philosophy is what you understand, learn and use; it is your personality that others understand.

612. A person's philosophy is his personality. If a person has no philosophy he is said to not have any personality.

613. The philosophy of God is divinity. The philosophy of a human being is humanity. The philosophy of a demon is monstrosity.

614. **Divinity:** is caused by truth, love, wisdom, faith, holiness, soul, morality, compassion, sacrifice, forbearance, delight, supernatural, uphold, heroism, mercy, donation, wonders, stability, relation with invisible powers, eternal life, miracles, victory, glory, impossibilities, immortality, good-natured, anger, prowess, exertion, chastity, peace, answer and forgiveness.

615. **Humanity:** is caused by discipline, hard work, fact, morality, love, relations, kindness, mercy, helping, wisdom, intelligence, trust, gratitude, donations, virtue, justice, correct behaviour, courage, happiness, delight, fear, responsibility, patience, arts, persistence, transformation, cleanliness, freedom, conscience and heart.

616. **Monstrosity:** - is caused by sacrificing others for own needs, cruelty, corruption, injustice, iniquity, violence, arrogance, pride, hatred, killing, conspiracy, cheating, exploitation, misdeeds, evil, selfishness, greed, lust, anarchy, disgust, illegality, immorality, hypocrisy, disobedience, having no gratitude, stupidity, and enjoying the suffering, difficulties and hardships of others.

617. Those who are inhuman and those who have monsters should not be compared to cattle and animals. Because they have a lot to learn from them.

618. A person with a personality understands a person who does not have a personality. Those who do not have personality hate persons who have personality.

619. You must have humanity to help others.

620. Being Good-natured is a good philosophy.

621. You cannot become a human being if you do not have humanity.

622. You must not reduce your humanity to improve your lifestyle.

623. Do not expect value and values from those who have no personality.

624. The stupidity of two types:

 1. Worrying about what is lost.

 2. Losing things that one is about to get.

625. Way to know personality – understanding the moral. The way to be good-natured is to follow the path of morals.

626. Personality depends on the philosophy of the person. Behaviour depends on the situation of the person.

627. Personality and habits are different. Personality decides life. Habits show the likes.

628. Personality does not depend on habits. Habits do not depend on personality.

629. A good habit will drive away another bad habit.

630. Attributes and symptoms are different and habits are different.

631. A person with good attributes can have bad habits. A person with bad attributes can have good habits. A person with bad attributes can have bad habits. A person with good attributes can have good habits.

632. Attributes: - Truth, love, exertion, mercy, holiness, good nature, morality, sacrifice, forgiveness and gratitude.
633. Symptoms: Good, bad, hate, anger, self-control, kindness, courage, concentration, reality.
634. Attributes are permanent; symptoms depend on the situation.
635. You get benefits until you have kindness in you.
636. Real ornaments of a person: Love, chastity, good nature, kindness, mercy.
637. Wearing ornaments is useless if you don't have chastity or self-respect in you.
638. The reason why men and women lose their chastity is – greediness and dissatisfaction.
639. If you have the characteristic of falsehood, it destroys your courage.
640. Your characteristic appears in your eyes.
641. The meaning of your thoughts can be understood by your look.
642. If you have the characteristic of truth in you, you have freedom.

-5-

Faith, Trust, Cheat

643. Trust is temporary; faith is forever.
644. Start a work only after you have faith that you can do it.
645. In this world, if you complete an impossible thing with faith, then you become a believer.
646. Faith gives obedience.
647. If you have faith, you can be courageous.
648. The most valuable things in this world are self-confidence and courage. If you feel they are needed then you can get them.
649. If a tree with life is cut down, it will come to life with budding. If you have faith, you will regain everything even if you lost everything.
650. Great deeds are possible by faith caused by the soul.
651. Your beauty does not give you self-confidence. Your beauty comes out because of your self-confidence.
652. The courage gained by faith is forever. Courage gained due to situations temporary.
653. Faith comes only after you experience despair.
654. Faith that is not implemented is like a sleeping body. Faith that is not implemented cannot stand.
655. Faith gives the power to face exertions, difficulties, dangers, problems, insults, blame and situations.
656. Depression comes because of fear.
657. A heart with no faith has depression.

658. Self-confidence is needed to overcome situations.

659. Strength, power, courage, patience and honesty come from faith.

660. Only, I can achieve – arrogance. I achieved – letting know, identity. I also can achieve – trust. I will achieve – faith.

661. It is a normal thing that someone cheats on you. It is easy for you to cheat others.

     It is difficult to make others trust you. It is a good thing that anyone trusts you. It is a great thing that anyone can keep faith in you.

662. Trust will occur on visible things. Faith will occur in invisible things.

663. Faith – will be on them who will give.

     Gratitude – is on those who already gave.

664. There are estimations for trust. There are no estimations for faith.

665. Trust occurs through sense organs. Faith occurs through the soul.

666. Trust is caused by everyone. Faith is caused to a few.

667. A few things that you do with a trust may or may not happen. Even if they happen, they are not glorified. But things are done with faith happen for sure and they cause praise and honour.

668. The path to regaining trust is – forgiveness and change of mind.

669. You should have belief in a person based on their deeds and not on their words.

670. When you tell a lie, you are suspected. When you tell lies you are mistrusted.

671. Give that much to a person as much as you trust him and expect that much from him.

672. Love everyone, but do not expect from and do not believe everyone.

673. Relationships without responsibility and trust cannot stand.

674. A thousand things can be told to those who believe. Do not tell the second thing to those who do not believe.

675. If you have no one who believes you, then you are a worthless person.

676. If you want to be trusted by at least one person, then you should not cheat on at least one person.

677. If you cheat anyone, it is cheating. If you cheat someone who believes you it is betrayal.

678. The reason why you lose trust:

    1. Underestimating others.

    2. Your greed.

    3. Because you have no patience.

679. Those who can cheat themselves can cheat anyone.

680. A person cheats on others only after cheating himself.

681. Those who cheat you:

    1. They will give more value to you.

    2. They will praise you and things that relate to you.

    3. They will show more and quick advantages.

    4. They will show love towards you without understanding you.

    5. Indirectly project themselves as great before you.

    6. They will show that they have more quantity of what you need.

    7. They will behave as if they do not like corruption.

    8. They get to know your strength and weakness.

682. People, who believe everything and get cheated many times, one day will believe a great thing and get that. Those who do not believe and want not to get cheated, lose the great thing that comes very rarely because they did not believe it.

-6-

Morality, Honesty, Reality, Fact

683. Whatever your thoughts are, your behaviour should have honesty and fact.
684. If you are honest, those who do well to you will get good and those who do harm you will get harm.
685. Not committing a mistake, even if there is a chance – is living honestly.
686. If you are honest, those who wish to harm you will feel shy; those who blame you get insulted.
687. If you have no honesty, you cannot do justice to any relationship.
688. If you are honest, you live with faith.
689. Anger with honesty is good.
690. Words without ethics may have meaning but have no value.
691. An effort that has no honesty may or not may get successful.
692. Ethics causes courage and faith. Sin causes cowardice and fear.
693. Ethics causes strength and success. Sin causes weakness and defeat.
694. Honesty is the measure of ethics.
695. Do not expect a full result from corrupt people.
696. Reality means being the same even when one may or may not have people, things, needs, power or money.
697. If you live in reality, you will lose what you do not need.
698. You will lose what you need if you continue living by pretending.

-7-

Love, Hate, Like, Dislike

699. Those who love you:

1. They will forgive your blunders, mistakes and weaknesses.

2. They will give you freedom and treat you the same as them.

3. They will tell you your faults and try to eliminate them.

4. They are ready to punish you or trouble you for your good.

5. They will serve you, and try to keep you happy and joyful.

6. They are ready to experience hardships and troubles for your sake.

7. They spend patience, tolerance, time, money and strength for your sake.

8. They try to make you into a strong and powerful one.

9. They even become ready to give their life to you if needed and if it is reasonable.

700. Those who hate you:

1. They will make fun of you and blame you based on your mistakes, blunders and weaknesses.

2. They will point out your blunders, mistakes and weaknesses to everyone.

3. They will try to waste your powers, facilities, money, time and strength.

4. They will try to cause difficulties, problems, harm or bad to you.

5. They will praise you, pretend to love you and do good to you.

6. They will pretend to help you or take help from you.

7. They will not be ready to give their money, time and things to you.

8. They will blame you, they conspire against you.

9. They will get ready to kill you.

701. There are two reasons for every activity that happens to human beings – love and hatred.

702. You will wholly experience either love or hatred when you are in a poor and worst condition.

703. A person, who has love will love his family, village, race, religion, state and country. He does as much good as he can.

704. A person who has hatred will hate other countries, states, religions, races, regions and other relations in his own family. And he harms them as much as he can.

705. Those who can control love and revenge can control anything.

706. Those who share love do not look for reasons. Those who use hatred look for reasons.

707. Love, truth and honesty are superior. These will give a superior status to a person.

708. Good and bad; like and dislike can be in the same person, but love and hatred cannot be in the same person.

709. Liking will be in everyone but love will not.

Anger will be in everyone but hatred will not.

710. However great you may be, if someone doesn't like you, they will not give value to you.

711. If you do not like yourself but are liked by others, it means that you are pretending.

712. If you don't like anything, say that you do not like it, but don't say it is not good, maybe someone else may say it's good.

713. Liking, desiring and obtaining are the stages to get something.

714. No matter how valuable it is, you look down on the things that you do not like, similarly however great you are, if they don't like you, they treat you in the same way.

-8-

Hope, Despair

715. Hope – is created irrespective of whether one has a qualification or not.

     Desire – is created which can be deserved.

716. Someone can fulfil your needs, but no one can fulfil your hopes and desires.

717. Do not hope to see the opportunities, have hope and search for opportunities. Only then will your work succeed.

718. Your strength and weakness will be known when you're in despair.

719. Despair is the foundation for hope.

720. You will know yourself only when you are in despair.

721. I must be good as per my power – is hope, one must have this. Must be good than anyone else – is greedy, one must not have this. Only I must be good – is greed, it is dangerous.

-9-

Aim, Ambition, Goal

722. Light to a dark room and a goal to an aimless life is essential.

723. You do not know what happens around you when you are sleeping. When you have no aim or any work, you do not know what happens in your life.

724. Your aim is light to your life; your practice is the path to it.

725. Your aim is your world; your practice is your fight for your kingdom and your aim.

726. You will get value because of your goal and credit because of your achievement.

727. How the more value of your ambition the lesser the value you will be to your opponents.

728. Life will be mechanical to those who have no aims, who learn nothing new and who cannot become change.

729. Your aim is created for yourself. Your ambition is created for others.

730. Your aim is more useful to you than to others.

731. Your ambition is more useful to others than you.

732. You are more valuable than your aim.

733. If you have an ambition, it is more valuable than you.

734. If you are living for yourself, you cannot pass time. If you live for your goal and ambition, time is not sufficient for you.

735. If you have any difficulty or a problem, get ready to suffer the results or have an ambition or a goal to overcome it.

736. Those who have no goal are equal to elders.

737. Things important to fulfil your ambition: truth, morals, faith, persistence, courage and planning.

738. If you have an ambition, and no one is criticizing, opposing or blaming you, it means that yours is not an ambition or it means that you are not doing anything for it.

739. Your mother did not stop giving birth to you fearing labour pains; likewise, you should not leave your goals and ambitions by fearing the hardships, exertions, obstructions and insults.

740. The reason why you are experiencing the problems is that you have no goal. If you have a goal, you have no time to experience problems.

741. Everyone has hope. It changes into a goal when it becomes stronger.

742. Food, sleep and comfort will become more valuable things to those who do have not any aim or ambition.

743. The deeds done with revenge, opposition, without any qualification and without being helpful to the poor are not ambitions, and these will not succeed.

744. Those who know what to expect from whom, and what is needed for the work can achieve anything.

745. Wisdom gives strength. Intelligence changes strength into power. Intelligence leads to achievement. Achievement makes a work successful. Successful work helps to achieve aim and ambition. Fulfilling aim and ambition leads to reaching the goal.

-10-

Strength, Weakness

746. The more you are crushed by the world, the more strength your soul gets.
747. The strength within you that you can see but the world cannot see is the strength of your soul.
748. If you utilize the strength in you, you become stronger.
749. If you use the weaknesses in you, you become weak.
750. Obstructions increase your strength.
751. You get strength depending on who strengthens you.
752. The strengths and weaknesses of something that you know can influence you.
753. Your strength is that you can know anything. Your weakness is, you feel that you know everything.
754. If you depend on your strength, you become a strong person. If you depend on the weaknesses of others, you will become a weak person.
755. Know your strengths from the persons, who took help from you. Know your weaknesses from the persons who helped you.
756. Things to follow to estimate a person fully:

    1. Their thoughts.

    2. Their words.

    3. Their deeds.

    The more the difference between them, the weaker they are. The less the difference between them, the stronger they are.

757. We become weak if we do things that should not be done. We become strong if we do things that should be done.

758. Not knowing is a weakness, not following even after knowing is powerlessness.

759. If weakness is high, it becomes slavery.

760. Sensitiveness and weakness are not the same.

-11-

Difficulty, Exertion, Blame, Patience

761. Difficulties in your life are opportunities to increase your ability.
762. You cannot become great by going through difficult times but you become great when you overcome them.
763. Those who cannot overcome situations can neither overcome difficulties.
764. Those who will change in favour of situations cannot change or overcome situations.
765. You completely experience neither comforts nor difficulties completely during your life stages like childhood, adolescence, adulthood, middle age and final stage.
766. Whatever sufferings, difficulties, exertions and insults you face can only destroy what you have, but cannot destroy you.
767. If you are lazy, you remain with hope. If you work hard, you will get the fruit.
768. Having difficulties at a young age is only for your good.
769. Those who come to you will come to you even in your difficulties, those who come for things that you have, come in your comforts only.
770. When you face difficulties, things and humans will go away from you which are not needed for you.
771. If you do not hard work, then you need to face some difficulties.
772. If you are suffering, it means you are learning something. If you are facing difficulties it means you are gaining strength.
773. Just like seasons, small difficulties will go and major difficulties will come, small happiness will go and big happiness will come.

774. Difficulties and comforts in life are like seasons; they keep coming and going.

775. Ways to get the ability to overcome difficulties and problems:

1. Create an aim or ambition to overcome them.

2. Spirituality.

776. Difficulties teach you patience. Patience teaches you achievement.

777. If you work hard for yourself that is your – hard work. If you work hard for others it is your – exertion.

778. Difficulties increase power. Sufferings increase strength.

Troubles give wisdom.

779. Suffering causes these two.

1. Change.

2. Revenge.

780. You should have only two answers to your hardships, troubles, burdens and insults – silence and a smile.

781. The person who has the ability to overcome hardships, troubles, and burdens will face them with a smile. Those who do not have the ability will suffer from anxiety.

782. Blame is a combination of a lie, false evidence, illegal work and a false explanation.

783. Blame is as strong as the person who slanders in terms of money, power and relation.

784. Blames will create and pushed as beliefs.

785. You should have self-confidence and live with morals to overcome blames.

-12-

Dare, Fear, Cowardice

786. If you have truth in you, it means you have courage.

787. Courage indicates your strength and power.

788. If you have the quality of falsehood, it spoils your courage.

789. You succumb to what you fear.

790. If you don't fear doing a wrong thing, you will have to fear when you have done a wrong thing.

791. Fear is of two types:

    1. The fear when doing something wrong.

    2. The fear when something wrong is done.

792. You will be scared when you have no strength. You will experience fear when you do not know about your strength. You will face fear when your strength is not of any use to you.

793. Fear – is what you experience when you do something knowing that it is wrong.

794. Cowardice – will not let you do anything even if you know it is good.

795. Fear and courage, both can be there in a person but cowardice and courage cannot be there in the same person.

796. You should have both fear and courage. Fear should be there to prevent mistakes.

    Courage should be there to do well. But cowardice should not be there.

797. Courage tells about your strength. Fear corrects your behaviour. Cowardice makes you weak and useless.

798. Desire is stronger than fear.

-13-

Season, Time, Feature, Past

799. Time stops for you only when you don't care for time.
800. Time heals pain and injury.
801. Take your own time to decide what to do; do not waste time after knowing what to do.
802. Time guides everything.
803. Time is the most valuable thing mostly available to everyone and the most wasted thing in this world.
804. Time is the most valuable thing that can be given by a person to others.
805. You must have faith to see the future.
806. The future never appears now.
807. Think about the future; then, you will have no time to think about the past.
808. If you want to grow up in life you should spend your time in the future.
809. The old thing will go when new things arrive. Don't think of what is lost; think and identify what is coming.
810. It is better to spend time-solving a problem than to worry about the problem.
811. Should learn from the past. Should have a plan for the future.
812. Your past deeds influence your present. Your present deeds influence your future.
813. You should learn from the past but don't think about it.

814. If you are talking about your past continually, it means you are leaving your future.

815. If you want to develop by thinking about things that happened in past, it is like walking to front while looking backwards.

-14-

Revive, Discipline

816. Because of reviving:

    1. You will think.

    2. You will have wisdom.

    3. You will be guided.

817. Revive is a combination of life, wisdom and action.

818. If you have discipline, you can understand yourself.

819. Two things appear in your behaviour: 1. Behavior with discipline. (or) 2. Animal behaviour.

820. Your discipline will remove a few obstructions and risks for you.

-15-

Work

821. You should consider work as penance.
822. If you are not doing any work, it means you are causing harm to yourself.
823. If you know what work to do and what not to do in right place, you will be called a good person, and if you don't know, you will be called a bad person.
824. Any work should be done with the heart first and then start with the body.
825. Before you start any work, you first need to get qualified for doing that work.
826. When doing work, focus on how, and why to do it and also on the result.
827. Learning is based on understanding. Skill is based on learning. The result is based on skill.
828. How much work you want to do is not important; what is important is how much you have done and what you have achieved.
829. Your value is not based on what you do but on your skill.
830. How the more patience and endurance inside you the more skillfulness will be in your work.
831. Any work you are doing with ethics will give better results.
832. Don't ever expect results from work which has no honesty and effort.
833. Don't do anything if you have no need or opportunity.

834. Don't do anything without liking it or if there is no need of doing it.

835. If you are not able to do what you want to do. Then do what you can.

836. To do the work, two things are required.

1. Thought.

2. Energy.

837. Works which are done with thoughts and without energy will be weak works and the result will be incomplete.

838. Works which are done without thought and with energy will be irrelevant works and the result will be hardships.

839. Reasons for a work to succeed: 1. Experience. 2. Ability. Both of these may or may not be there at the same time, at the same place.

840. If you don't have trust in what you do, none will trust you and your work.

841. Don't expect results from the work done by trusting others.

842. If the work is done with negligence, the outcome will be more loss than profit.

843. Money taken to do work is a bribe, which is not good.

Given work done - is a gift, which is not bad.

844. You must have both words and deeds. You must convince with words and fulfil with deeds.

845. You will get fame and a name from your professional life than your personal life.

846. Don't do the work that is good in this world, do the work which is good for you.

847. There will be two things that what to do and what not to do, in the work-doing process.

848. Punishments and results are of two types:

1. Those are caused due to not doing things that should be done.

2. Those are caused due to doing things that should not be done.

849. If you wish to live comfortably without doing anything, you become disabled at that very moment.

850. If you are doing others' work, without doing yours and your family's work, it means that you are cheating them.

851. If you are doing only your and your family's work, it means you are not fully performing your responsibilities.

852. If you are doing your work, your family's work and work for society, it means that you are fully performing your responsibilities.

853. If another person is doing your work it means:

    1. You are not able to do it.

    2. You are lazy

    3. The person who is doing it loves you.

854. If you do not manage what you should manage, others will manage it. If you don't do what you should do, others will do it. If you are not in the way you should be, then other person will be there in that place.

-16-

Victory, Win

855. Victory is achieving what you want. Winning is achieving what you want over others.
856. Victories are not those which are achieved unintentionally. Victories are those which are achieved intentionally.
857. Victory is preceded by problems. You cannot achieve victory if you fear problems.
858. Formula to achieve victory - your thoughts, words and deeds should remain the same without changing.
859. You become proficient when you can overcome impossible situations.
860. There will be Impossible situations before impossibilities. There will be problems before the victory.
861. Winning and honesty may or may not be there in the same place.
862. There will not be a victory for those who have no goals.
863. If you won with violence, only the win remains for you. If you won with love, you will gain things that are more valuable than winning.
864. If you need a kingdom, it's not important to be born to a king. Learning to fight and to win is important.
865. It doesn't mean it's a failure if you are defeated every time. When you stop making effort, then it is defeat.
866. Heroism does not depend on winning. It depends on fighting.

-17-

Good, Bad, Harm

867. If you are going down the wrong path, all the obstructions you get are good. If you are going in the good path, all the obstruction you get is bad.

868. Do not try to be called a good person. Try to be a good person. It is easy to be a good person.

869. Goodness is not bearing whatever others do, it is wishing well for others.

870. Do not expect good from opportunists.

871. Good and bad thoughts cannot live in you. Only one of those will live in you.

872. Wisdom will be born, when the evil and stupidity in you die.

873. All that appears good to you will not be good for you. Some of them may do bad.

     All that appears bad to you may not be bad for you. Some of them may do good.

874. Don't get spoiled by seeing others, others should see you and get inspired to become good.

875. When you do a great deed that this world can never imagine, then you may appear bad to this world.

876. Some deeds done by good people may appear bad to you, and some deeds of bad people may appear good to you. Observe the personality.

877. If someone envies you, stay away from them. There is nothing you can learn from them; you will get more bad from them than good.

878. You have to experience the fruits of what you love. If you love good things, you will experience good results. If you love bad things, you will experience bad results.

879. If more bad things happen to you than the good that you will do for others, then it is better not to do good.

880. Nothing is good or bad based on situations and limitations. Good are those which are subjected to limitations and situations. Bad are those which are not subjected to limitations and situations.

881. Things which are within limits are good. Things which cross the limits are bad.

882. Your discretion brings either a good or bad name to you.

883. If you underestimate others:

1. You will lose.

2. You will become bad.

884. If you help those who do bad deeds, then you are bringing bad to you also.

885. Selfishness is like a weapon. It can cause good or bad.

886. Losing is better than bad and harm.

887. Courage – lets you do good deeds.

Cowardice – stops you from doing good deeds.

Wickedness – lets you do bad deeds.

Fear – stops you from doing bad deeds.

888. If something bad happens to you because of yourself, it's your sin. If something bad is happening to others because of you, it is your vile.

889. It's better to be afraid before committing a mistake than after committing a mistake.

890. The people who are greedy deserve to be harmed.

891. Those who commit mistakes do not have the right to point out others' mistakes.

892. Prostitution is a bad thing. Corruption and betrayal are vile things.

893. If a person commits a mistake for needs, it is a mistake.

894. If a person commits an unnecessary mistake, it is meanness.

-18-

Envy, Hate

895. You feel Jealous of others if they possess something better than you. Envy develops when others have something that you do not have.

896. Learn from those who are in a better position than you; do not feel jealous. Know others who are not in a better position than you; do not make fun of them.

897. Jealousy and envy inside you can turn even your friends into enemies.

898. Reasons for a person to blame you:

 1. Your present status creates odiousness in him.

 2. Your present status creates jealousy in him.

899. What pests and insects do to a plant is what jealousy and hate will do to you.

900. If jealousy and hatred enter you, it means you are going to lose happiness and joy, and you will feel pain and hurt.

901. If you are not in a good position, you will be ridiculed and underestimated. If you are in a good position, you will face jealousy and hatred. If you live as you like, you will get delighted.

902. If you have jealousy and hatred, they will reduce your strength and increase your weaknesses.

903. Ways to control hatred:

 1. Service.

 2. Sports.

 3. Art.

904. People who hate you will do badly only to you even if you do good or bad to them.

905. Jealousy and hatred reside only in those who perform bad deeds.

906. Jealousy and hatred cannot reside in people who perform good deeds.

-19-

Relationships

907. A person has two types of relationships:

    1. Personal relations.

    2. Social relations.

908. In your life, relationships must influence you first. Then, other things must influence you.

909. When you lose everything, those who are with you are your friends and relatives. Those who feel bad – feel hurt when you are facing problems and hardships – they are your friends and relatives.

910. Those who are honest with you about your problems and comforts are your relatives, friends and loved ones.

911. With marriage, you will get a lifelong companion; do not ask for anything else. There is nothing more valuable than a companion.

912. Nothing is more valuable to you than you and your wife. If there is a dowry between you two, that will reduce your value.

913. It is more important to be parents than to be parents of either a boy or a girl.

914. Your parents are really honoured because of you, when others say that they want a child like you.

915. Have a friendship with good people or transform your friend to be a good person.

916. Relationships can have differences but not opposition.

917. Relationships will not survive where there is no responsibility and trust.

918. Your enemies are those who pretend as if they are not aware of you and your situation even though knowing very well. Never trust them.

919. Friendship and enmity depend on good and bad but not on caste, race, religion, region, education and money.

-20-

Money, Needs

920. If you think primarily about money, the world will appear bad to you. If you think primarily about love, you can understand that the world is good.

921. If you have money it does not mean that you have everything.

922. If you have no money, it does not mean that you do not have anything.

923. Money is permanent until the world exists, but you are not permanent. So, live for yourself.

924. Money fulfils your all needs but cannot solve your all problems.

925. If you need money, earn it without limits, but don't earn it by becoming a slave to money.

926. If you cannot speak about you earning money freely, it is not your earnings. It becomes your theft or your robbery or your cheating or betrayal.

927. Your earnings are those, which you can say freely that you earned.

928. There is no value for the money you earned if you don't donate some of it.

929. You will face problems if you don't value money; the problems will be as much as the greed of the world for money.

930. Money must be your need but not your weakness.

931. Your expenses must be in control, and so must be your need and be compulsory. There should be development, security and saving in your earnings.

932. You will get comfort, and happiness if you have money. If you have love, you will get delighted.

933. You need money to sustain. You need to have both money and love to live.

934. A human being is more valuable than time, money, education and power. Because all of these exist for human beings.

-21-

Comfort, Happiness, Delight, Romance

935. Comfort belongs to the body. Happiness belongs to the mind. Delight belongs to the heart.
936. That which you get on what you can see – happiness. That which you get on what you cannot see – delight.
937. You will become happy when you get something. You will be delighted when you give something.
938. Happiness is temporary. Delight is – permanent.
939. Happiness is what you will get when your hard work is useful to you. Delight is what you will get when your exertion is useful to others.
940. Happiness – when you get something. Sorrow – when you lose something. Delight – a permanent feeling that never goes away.
941. Delight will not occur to those who will give with expectations.
942. Happiness and sorrow cannot stay in the same place at the same time. But delight and sorrow can or cannot be in the same place at the same time.
943. Delight will be there in the work done. Happiness and sorrow will be there as a result of the work done.
944. People who search for temporary things for comfort and happiness lose the delight present in permanent things.
945. If you are remembering a person when you are happy and another person when you are in sorrow, then you will be a person with no values.
946. All the days that can keep you in delight are festive days.

947. If you want to be delightful, someone must be happy because of you.

948. Delight gives beauty but beauty cannot give delight.

949. Delight in your life does not depend on how much help you got; it depends on how much you helped.

950. A delight from truth, wisdom and love is permanent.

951. The reasons why there is a delight in your life are:

1. Because God is there in your life.

2. You have ambition.

3. Because you are honest.

952. You keep on losing delight while you living with pretention.

953. About sex:

1. It's not wrong for a woman and man who are mature physically and mentally to know about sex.

2. It's not wrong for a physically and mentally mature woman or man to have sex within limits, rules and with commitment.

3. There should not be cheating and betrayal in sex.

4. Sex gives comfort, happiness and children.

5. Irrelevant sex without limits and rules causes fear, anguish, loss, flimflam and unrest.

-22-

Help, Donation

954. Giving to those who you need is need.

     Giving to those who need to be with you is helpful.

     Giving to those who cannot give back to you is a donation.

955. The help you do to those you want has no value. The help you do to others who are in need of you – is valuable. Helping people who have a goal and purpose is the greatest one.

956. There is no need for friendship, love and a relationship between two people to help. There should be humanity in them.

957. Don't remain an advisor; become a person who also helps.

958. Don't worry that others are not helping you. Feel delightful by helping others.

959. Helping others is a habit that you should possess compulsorily.

960. Help those who want to develop and not those who want to be comfortable.

961. Do not waste the help that you get.

962. If you misuse the help that you received from others, both you and the other, who helped, will lose.

963. You feel happy when the help you received is put into good deeds, and also makes the person who helped you delightful.

964. You will get help based on the person you are depending on.

965. You can expect help from others but cannot depend on others.

966. Incapable are those who do not help even when they are capable.

967. Worse are those who treat helping people as workers.

968. Your service and help should not be forced one; they should be voluntary.

969. Real donation is given to those who cannot return it.

970. Donation is not giving things that you do not need. It's about giving what others need.

971. Donating to people who already have can never be a donation.

972. People who know only to take and who do not know to give remain as lower people.

973. Those who depend only on others and help only others will lose themselves.

974. Those who want to take without the knowledge of those giving, and get things done without the knowledge of those doing are dangerously selfish people and unknown enemies.

-23-

Angry, Audacious, Proud, Arrogance

975. Anger, audacity, pride and arrogance are not the same.
976. Pride and arrogance are not needed. Anger and audacity are needed.
977. One must be audacious to answer arrogant people. One must have anger to control unsystematic people.
978. Valour is your additional qualification.
979. If someone is angry with you, it will go at some point. But if someone disgusts you, it will remain forever.
980. If you commit a mistake once, others will be angry with you. If you repeat the same mistake, others will feel disgusted about you.

-24-

Your, To You, You, Thee, Yours

981. You cannot know about others until you know yourself.
982. There may be many people greater than you, but there should not be anyone you like more than yourself.
983. Your value will be as less when your deeds are less than your words.
984. Your greatness will not be in underestimating others, it will be in understanding others.
985. A person with negative thoughts cannot think positively about you.
986. Do not keep your faults that you know, until others point them out.
987. The more you can control your senses, the more powerful you will become.
988. If you cry for your misfortune, you will be ruined.
989. If you are living according to the world and not according to what your soul expects, it is your self-deceit.
990. If your soul wants to do something and you do not let your body cooperate, it is will be your deceit.
991. Do not expect everyone to be like you. Do not think that everyone will be like you. Do not expect everyone to be like someone. Do not think that someone will be like another one.
992. Solitude is not having anyone around you.
993. Loneliness is not having a relationship with people around you.
994. Do not neglect yourself. Likewise, do not neglect others also.

995. Expect your right after performing your responsibilities.

996. It is your responsibility to support lowly, weak and powerless people.

997. Life is more important to you than good food. A good body is more important than good clothes.

998. Things that you need alone are valuable. Things that you do not need, however valuable they are, are a waste to you.

999. If you focus on things like power, education, body, money, food and comfort, which you can see, you cannot get invisible things like life, love, hunger and happiness. If you focus on invisible things, you can gain visible things also.

1000. If you value those who don't value you, you will have suffering, anguish, deceit, betrayal and blame.

1001. You might face adverse conditions, but if you stand strong, they will cross you.

1002. Your pain does not depend on your injury; it depends on the situation you got injured.

1003. You may not know everything but can know anything.

1004. Powers can be helpful to you but they are not visible.

1005. Waiting is needed for you. While you are waiting, you will gain the qualification required for what you are waiting for.

1006. You will know new things until you die. Don't ever get the feeling that you know everything.

1007. If you are human, nothing is more valuable to you than yourself.

1008. The village you were born in is not yours. The caste you were born into is not yours.

1009. If you keep pretending to change, you cannot enjoy the delight that comes with change.

1010. You may or may not believe people who are silent but do not underestimate them.

1011. You have to consider only these two as your enemies:

1. Those who cause danger to your life.
2. Those who obstruct your path.

1012. When you are not able to follow, whatever you hear will go waste.

1013. You belong to the thing that you succumbed to.

1014. You cannot learn everything but can learn anything.

1015. Even if you see obstruction and defeat in the path of achieving something, do not adopt untruth.

1016. Before estimating others, first, know whether you have that qualification or not.

1017. You cannot change others until you do not change.

1018. If you need it or not, if it is valuable or not, if you don't give value to something, it will go away from you.

1019. If you give value to something, it stays with you. Even if it is useful to you or not, even if it has value or not.

1020. You won't get respect from a person to whom you give no value.

1021. Do not expect value from someone whom you do not give value to.

1022. Expecting value from a person to whom you don't give value is arrogance.

1023. It is important to know how you are and it is also important to know what type of people you are with.

1024. You underestimating others will not make them lowly people. Your overestimating others will not make them great.

1025. If you keep on thinking of using others, you will fall. If you keep thinking about how to be useful to others, you will develop.

1026. If something you want does not happen, it might be harmful to you; if something you do not want happens, it might have benefited you.

1027. You may or may not keep something that is given by someone else. But you can definitely keep what you earned.

1028. Do not try to get anything for free. Try to get it as a reward.

1029. You can do what you want and what you intended only when you are being as you are.

1030. Your lips will tell what you are speaking out. Your eyes will tell what you are thinking.

1031. If you are clean, it means you are clean. If your surrounding is clean, it means you are hygienic.

1032. You are not going to be great in a day or a year.

1033. A real qualification for you to see this world is you can look into yourself.

1034. Think when you are giving a promise to someone; do not think when you are fulfilling it.

1035. If you do not change, you cannot develop.

1036. When you do not know that you can scare this world with the courage to die, only then you will do suicide.

1037. If you get a thought that nobody gets, it needs to be fulfilled by you, not others.

1038. It is not important how the world sees you, it is important how you see yourself.

1039. You are one in this world; you are not a slave to this world.

1040. Things you have to do to win yourself:

    1. Not cheating others.

    2. Not cheating yourself.

1041. If you underestimate yourself, your ability is wasted.

1042. There is a selfish thought behind everything that human beings do. It may or may not do good to you.

1043. Self-respect is liking yourself honestly and really.

1044. To say that something belongs to you, it must not belong to others.

1045. If anything belongs to you that:

1. Must belong only to you. or
2. Must be earned by you. or
3. Must be created by you.

-25-

Other Sentences

1046. Criticizing and opposing are two different things.

1047. Criticism is not acceptable or unacceptable.

1048. Explanation eliminates doubts. Argument builds doubts.

1049. Pity is of two types:

1. Others show pity on you.
2. You show pity on yourself.

1050. If others show pity on you, it is the situation. If you pity yourself, it is a bad situation.

1051. Imitation comes from what is visible. Adaptation comes from what is invisible.

1052. Adaptation is greater than imitation.

1053. When all the paths are closed, a new path will open.

1054. To get redemption needs to hope.

1055. By following orders, one will get more benefits than damages.

1056. Valuable things for a man:

1. Firstly, his heart.
2. Next is his time.
3. After that, his money.

1057. Reasons for problems:

1. Not having knowledge.
2. Not having patience.

3. Trying to cover mistakes without correcting them.

4. Being a bad person and trying to be called a good person by others.

1058. Decisions are not correct when the opinions and estimations are not correct.

1059. If you hurt someone by establishing a reason, the same reason will hurt you.

1060. It does not matter whether a valueless person gives value to you or not.

1061. A tree does not die even if the leaves all fall down; it gains leaves, flowers and fruits when spring comes.

1062. To get the best things, one must eliminate things that are not the best.

1063. Science is a path that man has created to know things in this creation, but science is not a creation.

1064. Education is not only for employment. It is for knowledge, development and employment.

1065. Your enemy is the one who fights in front of you. He will cause loss. Opponents are those who stay beside you and wish to harm you. Because of them, both loss and destruction will happen.

1066. If you are moving in a path, there are people who pull you back, and who lead you backwards. Likewise, there are people who push you forward, and who lead you forward.

1067. Insult happens to you only when you accept it; you are not insulted if someone insults you.

1068. You need to find wealth, and should not rob it.

1069. If you don't want to grow, it does not matter how great those who try to make you grow are.

1070. Even if you are a stone, if you shine, you become a pearl. If you share lighting, you become a diamond.

1071. Only people who have fear will show discrimination and be subjected to discrimination.

1072. Experience comes with effort. Ability comes with practice.

1073. A person is not inferior or superior to any other person. Superiority and inferiority will be in their bodies, thoughts, words and deeds only.

PART THREE

LOVE, FRIENDSHIP

-1-

Love, Like, Friendship

1074. The source of all relations is love.

1075. The thing that you get from all relations and shared with all relations is love.

1076. If you feel love, you should express it. But by letting others know, you will not get love into yourself and the person you love.

1077. Love those who don't love you, but don't give value to those who don't give value to you.

1078. Proof that you have love inside you is that every living being appears valuable to you.

1079. If you have no love for yourself, you cannot love others.

1080. The purpose of love is not staying together; it is in giving a good life to the person you love by you or others.

1081. If there is love in you, you can forgive those who you love.

If you have no love in you, you cannot forgive those who you like.

1082. Value for your love is not based on how much you gave to the person you love. Value for your love is based on how much you lost for them.

1083. The one who loves you is a gift to you; you are the gift to the one whom you love. Days and gifts are not more valuable than you.

1084. If you feel love for anyone or if anyone tells you that they love you, you first need to understand what is love.

1085. If your mate loves you, your life will be happy. If your mate wants what you have, your life will remain incomplete.

1086. Change your mate to the way you like, but do not love everyone you like as your mate.

1087. Those who love you can change themselves as you like, but all those whom you like do not love you.

1088. Share your love with those who love you but do not lose your life.

1089. Those who do not understand you are not those who love you.

1090. Those who love you cannot cheat you. People who cheat on you cannot love you.

1091. Love is very strong and powerful; only people who are honest can afford and continue it.

1092. If you understood what love is, then you will know how to love and whom to love. A person who has love can share his love based on his ability with his parents, wife and children, relatives, friends and society.

1093. Love can happen to anyone, but will be fulfilled only in those who have facts and honesty.

1094. If two lovers believe each other, it is related to those two. If there is faith between two lovers, it is related to love.

1095. Love is related to two hearts; marriage is related to two bodies. If both of these happen with one person, then both happiness and delight will be there.

1096. If love creates a bond between two people, their love and relationship stay even if they are not together. Those who got to unite for love; will have a relationship only when they are together.

1097. If love unites someone, nothing can separate them except love.

1098. Anything and anyone can separate the people who feel they are in love.

1099. Love does not succumb to situations, needs, hardships and insults.

1100. What is born after understanding each other is not love. It is understanding.

What makes you understand each other after having love is love.

1101. Love creates faith, hope and patience in a person.

1102. Unconditional, boundless and everlasting is love.

1103. There are no changes or differences in love.

1104. There will be changes and differences in those who love.

1105. Lovers who cannot stay apart for one year cannot live together even for one year.

1106. The most powerful and strong thing is that which loves others. Those who are able to do this can do anything.

1107. Those who cannot love themselves cannot love anyone, anything.

1108. There will be remaining cheating when you love someone who has cheating attributes.

1109. Loving those who don't have personality causes nonsense and unwanted things to those who love them.

1110. Those who have no love can say that they love, but they cannot love.

1111. Those who have love will like someone who has love even in any situation.

1112. Love and relationship are two different things.

1113. Relationship without love is lifeless.

1114. Don't expect love from those who do not have love.

1115. One can get love from those who have love.

1116. Those who have love can love everyone.

1117. Those who do not have love cannot love anyone.

1118. Responsibility or pretention will be in a relationship which has no love.

1119. Giving does not increase the value of love. Not giving doesn't reduce the value of love.

1120. Everyone will not express or show love in the same way.

1121. There is no need for people who have love to expect love from others.

1122. Those who have love can love others and share it. But will not expect from others.

1123. Greed and greedy will not be present in those people who have love.

1124. People who have loved have faith, patience, endurance, sacrifice, forgiveness, service and kindness.

1125. People who have love will not have hatred. But they may have revenge and avenging.

1126. People who have loved have both love and relationships. People who do not have love have only relationships.

1127. Love has a language.

1128. There is no fear in love.

1129. By waiting, love will increase.

1130. Punishment with love becomes training.

1131. Love is to live, just like life is to the body.

1132. Disgusting and love cannot stay together in one place.

1133. If you don't have love, your life will be wasted.

1134. People who do not know love name its innocence.

1135. Only those who do not know about love try to decide it in one day.

1136. Love is life but the love of young men and women is not life.

1137. Love is not something that happens when we see others. It is what you get from those who have love, and it is what is in you and shared with others.

1138. When we see others, we will feel affection, liking and emotion. When we stay with others, we will feel closeness; relationships and feelings are created.

1139. Appearance causes liking. The behaviour causes – affection. What comes from you – love.

1140. Affection and liking are temporary. Love is – forever.

1141. What comes from others is – liking and affection. What comes from you is love.

1142. Liking will be there only if the appearance is good. Liking remains only when the behaviour is good. Love remains in any condition.

1143. There will be a delight when there is love between two people. There will be happiness when there is a liking between two people. There will be a comfort when two people are together.

1144. You will feel sad if you lose the person you like. You will lose the relationship if you lose the person you love.

1145. Love is universal. Liking is personal.

1146. People who have love should marry honest people. People who don't have love should marry a person who has the things they like.

1147. People who have love can love everyone, but don't like everyone. People who don't have love cannot love anyone; they like only those whom they like.

1148. Someone will like the people who have the things that they like.

1149. Someone may like others more than themselves. But they cannot love others more than themselves.

1150. Liking is like receiving. Love is like giving.

1151. A relationship with like will have happiness, problems and suffering. A relationship with love will have delight, forgiveness and faith.

1152. If you like, you will expect; if you love, you will submit.

1153. Everyone can like, but everyone cannot love.

1154. Liking may be there in everyone, but love will not be in everyone.

Anger may be there in everyone, but hatred will not be there in everyone.

1155. Liking occurs from others. Affection occurs from others. Love will get from others. But love does not happen when seeing others.

1156. Love and friendship are very valuable. Those who don't know the value will use these for self desires. Those who know the value become useful to these.

1157. One should lose money and bodily desires for love and friendship. But do not use the words love and friendship for money and bodily desires.

1158. The strength of love and friendship is that they can forgive the bigger mistakes, but can't withstand even little betrayal.

1159. People who make friends or liking with expecting something, cannot enjoy love and friendship.

1160. People who don't have love cannot do justice to love and friendship.

1161. Love can be shown to everyone but friendships cannot be had with everyone.

1162. There will not be love in all those who have a friendship. All those who have friendship cannot love.

1163. Love is universal. A friendship is personal.

1164. A person cannot increase or decrease the value of love and friendship.

1165. Your friends are those who think about what they can give you. Those who expect something from you will not be your friends.

1166. You will be comfortable with the right friend. You will grow with the friend who corrects you.

1167. Those who don't understand you because of your faults are not your friends.

1168. Going with a person for your needs is – debauchery. Spending time with a person whose attitude is like you is – friendship.

1169. Friendship is one of the many relations.

1170. They are not your friends if they cannot see you as yourself.

1171. People who have no self-respect and conscience cannot be friends.

1172. Two people who have a conscience can live together. Two people who do not have a conscience can live together. But one person has a conscience and another having no conscience cannot reside and live together.

1173. For people to live together, they must possess faith, patience, endurance and sacrifice in them.

1174. A man and woman become a couple due to three things: love, friendship and lust. The reason how they become a couple is known based on what they do. Every couple is not a loving couple.

1175. If a woman and a man are becoming a couple:

1. Due to lust, they can only unite their bodies.
2. Due to friendship, they satisfy the needs of one another.
3. By due to love, they live for each other.

PART FOUR

SOCIETY

-1-

Truth, Justice, Virtue

1176. There are no alternatives to truth, justice and virtue.

1177. Untruth is that which is not true. Iniquity is that which is not a virtue. Injustice is that which is not justice.

1178. Untruth prevails where there is no truth. Iniquity prevails where there is no virtue. Injustice prevails where there is no virtue.

1179. A person may end his life without knowing what is love and truth.

1180. People who have a conscience will accept the truth. People who don't have a conscience cannot accept the truth.

1181. Things like to me and to us only are commitments, but not theories, virtues and truths. And these things will not apply to all people.

1182. Allowing every qualified person is justice.

1183. Giving superiority to those who are superior is a virtue.

1184. Justice and virtue never lose their value.

1185. Those who can follow justice and virtue will have value.

1186. Those who cannot follow justice and virtue will not have value.

1187. Real incapability is compromising with injustice and dishonesty.

1188. Virtue is of two types:

   1. Giving superiority to those who are superior.

   2. Strong people give support to weak people.

1189. Where there is no justice, differences will be there. Where there is no virtue, inequalities will be there.

1190. Virtue will not be there where there is no justice.

1191. Those who cannot live honestly cannot live as a virtue.

-2-

Society, World, System

1192. Why will society change unless you change? Society changes only if you change.

1193. If you are one in society, do something good for society according to your capacity.

1194. If you are responsible towards society, society will respect you.

1195. Students and youth should have these two mandatory responsibilities:

   1. Understanding society.

   2. Making society good.

1196. Everyone in society is born a human, but everyone does not live like humans.

1197. Living in society happily, joyfully, and respectfully does not mean living without doing any hard work.

1198. In society, there are people who are in good condition and there are people who are in bad conditions.

1199. There are both people who are good and who pretend to be good in this society.

1200. Need has more value than goodness in this society.

1201. Society will not respect those who have no responsibility towards society.

1202. Society does not give value to those who do not give value to society.

1203. To live in society, intelligence and money are required. To change society, wisdom and faith are required.

1204. Those who want to change society without changing themselves will fail.

1205. There are two types of people in society who are happy:

Those who earn in wrong routes, earn by cheating and by gaining illegally.

Those who earn with honesty, integrity and legally.

1206. The social life of people depends on the government. The personal life of people is based on race and customs.

1207. The life of people who want to avoid problems in this society and want only comfort will become hell. The life of people who faces hardships through living in this world with ethics and in reality will become heaven.

1208. This world fears only those who are not afraid of this world.

1209. The system always wants change but it cannot change. Human beings can change but are not changing. The system changes only when human beings change.

1210. Good and bad will not be in professions, systems and regions, it is in persons.

1211. Systems will not spoil; the people in the systems will spoil.

1212. A person cannot love the country by hating people.

1213. There will not be patriotism for those who have no humanity.

1214. Humanity is greater than patriotism.

-3-

Wisdom, Ignorance, Intelligence, Stupidity

1215. Wisdom is the origin of theories.

1216. Change with intelligence is temporary. Change with wisdom is revolutionary.

1217. Everyone has intelligence. Only a few have wisdom.

1218. People who have wisdom will explain. People who have ignorance will argue.

1219. Explanation eliminates doubts. Argument builds doubts.

1220. People who have wisdom never want or encourage violence.

1221. One can be intelligent but may lack wisdom. One may have intelligence and knowledge but not wisdom. One may have intelligence, knowledge and wisdom.

1222. Intelligence is that which every living being generally gets for survival. Knowledge is that which comes from past and present things around oneself. Wisdom is that gained by a person by himself, for himself.

1223. Every living being has intelligence. Only human being has wisdom.

1224. Hatred cannot reside in the people who have wisdom. Hatred can reside in only the people who have ignorance.

1225. Ignorant people are psychologically blind.

1226. Main characteristics of an ignorant person:

    1. He feels that he knows everything.

    2. He feels that others don't know as much as he knows.

1227. Untruths will create by ignorance and opportunism.

1228. People who think that others will be just like what they estimate are ignorant people.

1229. The deeds are done by ignorant people:

1. They will not be creative
2. There will not be development.
3. They will not be honest.

1230. Ignorant people waste their time.

1231. People who spend time with ignorant people also waste their time.

1232. Ignorant people cannot identify or assess the future.

1233. People who argue without having a conscience are stupid; those who argue with them are also stupid.

1234. Superstition is:

1. Thinking that the same thing may happen again and again.
2. Thinking that what happened to a person might happen to everyone.

1235. It is stupidity to repeatedly try to change a stupid person.

1236. A wise man gets to know at least a second time. That is why he will become good.

1237. A stupid person pretends as if he knows it; that's why he falls.

1238. Change is for those who want to change and who want change, but not for stupid people.

-4-

Morality, Corruption, Good, Bad

1239. All those who are involved in corruption are not wicked, they are weak. They engage in corruption because of a lack of power. Righteous people are not incapable; they are powerful. Since they are powerful, they do not engage in corruption.

1240. Righteous people will appear good to good people and bad to bad people.

1241. Bad people suffer their whole life. Righteous people suffer only until they find the path of righteousness.

1242. All people who do good deeds are not good. Only the people with a good heart are good.

1243. Only those who do good to others are good people.

1244. Opportunists are those who do good to a few people and bad to a few people.

1245. The life of those who do bad, damage and harm to others gets destroyed.

1246. Not doing bad to others is a good quality. Doing good to others is a great quality.

1247. Good comes out slowly where there are more bad things. Good things happen late where bad is strong.

1248. Good may happen or may not happen from those who cannot identify what is good and from those who want good to happen only through them. Bad things may happen because of them. These two can or cannot be in the same person.

1249. People who commit mistakes by creating causes and opportunities are bad people.

1250. Good people search for good even in a bad thing. Bad people search for bad even in a good thing.

1251. When there are no good paths, or if good paths are unknown, people will follow the bad path.

1252. Bad things will happen to those who harm others even though they have good habits. Good things happen to those who do good to others even though they have bad habits.

1253. Those who do not know what is good and bad are not bad people. Those who do bad things even though they know about good and bad are bad people.

1254. To do good things, there is no need for any reason. But reasons are needed to do bad things. That is why reasons are searched for before doing something bad.

1255. Those within limits are good and those who cross the limit are bad.

1256. Those who possess bad things cannot focus on good things.

1257. Bad people and spoiled people are not the same.

1258. There is no need for spoiled people to feel suffering, grief and anguish. It's their responsibility to become good again.

1259. Those who like bad deeds are bad people. Those who like good deeds are good people.

1260. Friendship with incapable and weak people is better than friendship with bad and wicked people.

1261. Some people possess that much love which can bring life. Some people possess so much hatred that can kill.

1262. The vile thing that a human can do is – to kill a person who does no harm to him.

The most degrading thing that a human can do is harm a person that did no harm to him.

1263. More time is needed for people who harm others.

1. To establish a reason to do it.
2. To do it.
3. To cover it.

1264. Degraded and weak are those who commit and cover their mistakes.

1265. Courage will be there to do good in people who are scared to commit a mistake.

1266. Wicked are those who give value to the words of a wicked person.

1267. Fearing wicked people is also wickedness.

1268. If any people oppose the people who are practising the truth, they are definitely either weak, wicked, bad or vile.

1269. People who commit mistakes are weak. People who do harm are vile.

1270. People who blame others even after losing the qualification to get forgiveness are wicked.

1271. Sinners are those who think evil, speak evil and do evil and expect good to happen to them.

1272. Only wicked people can betray, be deceitful and conspire. Only weak people can lie and cheat.

1273. Wicked people do not have calmness, peace and answer.

1274. If they do it intentionally or unintentionally:

1. People who engage in corruption are corrupted people.
2. People who do betray and cheat are traitors.
3. People who conspire and betray are vile people.
4. People who do murder and who plan murders are both murderers.

1275. Bad people have no peace of mind even when things happen as they intended or even if things don't happen.

1276. The unity of wicked people leads to destruction for themselves or others. The unity of righteous people leads to good for themselves or others.

1277. The unity of righteous people is greater than the unity of wicked people.

1278. People who have no conscience will cheat themselves and others.

1279. People who have no conscience will do and make others do contrasting deeds.

1280. People who have self-respect cannot deceive themselves. People who do have not self-respect can deceive themselves.

1281. The intelligence of righteous people is powerful and greater than the intelligence of corrupt people.

1282. Violence is the main and primary path for cruel people.

1283. Harm and destruction come suddenly to the people who do not listen even though given a warning, who do not change their behaviour even though given a chance and who try harming others again and again.

1284. Living with unrest is also a result of harm.

1285. Righteous are those who correct their mistake and try not to repeat them.

Wicked people are those who cover their mistakes and repeat mistakes to justify themselves.

1286. Those who have love will feel happy by doing welfare. Those who have hatred will feel happy by doing harm.

1287. Those who want to be known as great person show what they have to others.

Great people share what they have with others.

1288. Normal people are those who do good to people who do good to them. Lower are those who forget about the good and people who did it. Vile are those who do bad to people who do good to them. Great are those who do good to people who do bad to them.

1289. The right to punish bad people will only be available to those who protect good people.

1290. All those who experience difficulties cannot become great. Only those who overcome difficulties become great.

1291. Great people have good characteristics, but all those with good characteristics cannot become great people.

1292. One cannot become great until one accepts great things. Things that are not useful to others can never become great things. Those who are of no use to others cannot become great.

1293. People who have sacrificed courage can definitely perform good deeds.

1294. Insects and animals cannot become greater than human beings even though they kill human beings. A person can never become a great person in society by killing another person.

-5-

Self-Confidence, Self-Respect

1295. People who do not have self-confidence will live subjected to situations. People with self-confidence will live beyond situations.

1296. People who have no faith will compare themselves with others and depend on others.

1297. Humans are of two types:

    1. Those who have self-respect.

    2. Those who have opportunism.

1298. Those who are not honest do not have self-respect.

1299. There is no value for a person who has no self-respect.

1300. Those who have no self-respect cannot give value to others.

1301. People with no self-respect have opportunism.

1302. People with no self-respect have no respect except for opportunism.

-6-

Ens, Personality

1303. Giving value to a person and not giving any value to his personality and thoughts, does not like him but it is a necessity.

1304. People who have no personality will compare themselves with others.

1305. Not allowing a man to live like a human being is a monstrosity.

1306. Psychologically disabled persons depend on others and have jealousy.

1307. There is no value for people who have no personality.

1308. The wants of two persons can be the same, but the personality of two persons might not be the same. The personality of two people can be the same but their wants might not be the same.

1309. If you want to know about a person, find out what he knows.

1310. A personality that does not succumb to gold and money is greater than gold and money.

1311. There is no value if the eye has no vision and man has no humanity.

1312. The philosophy of a person is called his personality.

1313. If the philosophy of a person is divinity, he is a man of God. If the philosophy of a person is human, he is a human being. If the philosophy of a person is monstrosity, then he is a humanoid monster.

1314. People who do have not a personality will not give value based on personality; they will give value based on necessity.

1315. The bigger the difference between the words and deeds of a man, the more he is not trustworthy.

1316. Those who have no humanity cannot live like human being. Those who have humanity can live like human being.

1317. Good thoughts are good personalities. Good personalities are good human beings.

Good human beings are a good society. Good societies are good countries. Good countries become a good world.

-7-

Life

1318. There are endless happiness and feelings in the life of humans. These occur only when they live like human beings.

1319. No one has the right to command the life of a person before or after he is born.

1320. Traditions and cultures are not more valuable than human beings because they are made for human beings.

1321. There are people who live like human beings. There are people who pretend as human beings.

1322. People who live with pretending will lose themselves.

1323. A few people may have happiness and comfort, but may not have life and future. A few people may have a life and future, but may not have happiness and comfort.

-8-

Caste, Religion, Area, Culture

1324. A human being is more valuable than caste, religion, region and culture because they all are made for him.

1325. Persons with hatred only bring a bad name to the country, religion, culture, and race they are born to or are following.

1326. People who are involved in caste and religion will lose their freedom and independence.

1327. Humans are those who live beyond region, religion, caste and money.

1328. The people who have hatred use caste, religion, money and race to hate others.

1329. The reason why caste and religion are considered bad is that humans use them to hate others.

1330. Caste is untruth. If it is true, it will be everywhere.

1331. Caste is a norm, but it is not the truth.

1332. There are no region, caste, race, gender or age differences to good-bad and morality-immorality.

1333. Those who have no conscience and self-respect will become slaves to persons, money, religion, caste or norms.

1334. Those who have hatred are the same even though which region, race, religion, or caste they follow. All those who have loved are the same even though they differ by region, race, religion or caste.

1335. Region, religion, caste, money and power cannot influence those who live with honesty.

1336. It does not matter to whom and where a person is born; his personality will be based on the place and situation in which he grows.

1337. Religion is related to personal life. A profession is related to social life.

1338. There is no need for society to know about the religion of a person but society must know the profession of a person.

1339. Religion and culture are not the same. People with many religions are there is one culture. People with many cultures are there in one religion. Cultures, religions and spiritual paths are not the same.

-9-

Leadership

1340. A leader is a servant to many people.

1341. A leader is one who leads others.

1342. Leadership qualities come from difficulty and comfort but not from dynasty, money and education alone.

1343. A leader must have sacrifice, courage, planning, honesty, impartiality, vision, discretion, knowledge, hard work, patience, endurance, perseverance, punctuality, the strength of talking and accuracy.

1344. Leadership is not related to dominance; it is related to responsibility.

1345. Leaders will not have professions, they will have only destinations.

1346. Those who want to be useful to others are leaders. Those who want to use others are cheaters.

1347. Those who cannot work for others cannot become leaders. People with partiality cannot become leaders. People with partiality are not leaders.

1348. People who have no leader will become degenerates.

-10-

Marriage

1349. Marriage is not just the union of men and women; it is the union of two hearts.

1350. Personality, faith and love are the important things needed for marriage.

1351. The main qualifications needed for bride and bridegroom for marriage:

Bridegroom:

1. Good heart to love wife.
2. The power to support the wife.
3. Forgiveness and conscience.
4. Patience and endurance to face problems and comforts.

Bride:

1. Good heart to love husband.
2. Obedience to the husband.
3. Forgiveness and conscience.
4. Patience and endurance to face problems and comforts.

But not religion, region, caste, profession or money.

1352. In marriage, men can allow what the woman brings, but should not expect anything to allow a woman to come to him.

1353. One should not take dowry, because it becomes the value of man. There is nothing more valuable than a man.

1354. When a woman has beauty and charm, people praise her – this is useless.

When a woman brings a good name to her husband, she is praised – this is needed.

1355. A man or a woman can seek freedom but should not behave according to will.

A man or woman can seek equality but should not show dominance.

1356. Things husband and wife should have after marriage:

1. Surrender themselves to each other.
2. Love without any suspicion.
3. Having fear and discretion about their behaviour.
4. Amiable behaviour.
5. Doing good to each other.
6. Having courage towards each other.
7. Having friendships only with good people.

1357. Out of husband and wife, at least one should follow ethics. Otherwise, their children will be spoilt.

1358. Women and men both are not one; they become one only when they are together.

-11-

Needs, Money, Poverty, Corruption

1359. The needs of a person depend on his body, thoughts and situations.

1360. People who look for others to meet their needs cannot build their future.

1361. The needs of everyone are not the same and will not be similar.

1362. It is not people without money who have no right to live on this earth, but those who cannot live like human beings.

1363. Having more money is dangerous.

1364. A real beggar is one who expects from others even if they have the things.

1365. Poor are those who do not donate even if they have things.

1366. People who do not pay the workers are poorer than workers.

1367. Money is not bad; humans are becoming bad for the money.

1368. Society gives quick recognition to wealthy men and beautiful women. It is not their greatness.

1369. Poverty is not having opportunities; necessitous is the inability to use opportunities. There are hardships in poverty but there can be happiness.

1370. An increase in prices only means corruption and poverty are increasing.

1371. Corruption and poverty are internal enemies of a person or a country.

1372. Corruption belongs to people; it has to be eradicated by them. Poverty belongs to society and anyone can eradicate poverty of anyone.

-12-

Work, Exertion, Development

1373. People who help and who work are not the same.

1374. Reasons for a person not doing work:

    1. Not having the ability to do it.

    2. Not having the interest to do it.

1375. Development and delight will not be in the work done expecting results.

1376. There is no great work than the cultivation of food, which is the primary need of all.

1377. Work is needed for all and those who do that work are great.

1378. Workers, labourers and employees are the soldiers that run the lifecycle. We must be thankful to them.

1379. Reasons why a person works for others:

    1. Because he loves them.

    2. Because of needs.

    3. Because of slavery.

1380. A person must be valued not based on his work, but based on his skills.

1381. There will not be any useless people; there are only people who are not able to do all things.

1382. The development will be there where will be the value to labour and labourer.

1383. Any race that cannot develop can never survive.

1384. Those who look after only themselves or look after only others can never develop.

1385. The reason why a person cannot develop:

1. Overestimating the situation they are in.
2. Underestimating themselves.

1386. People who do have not discipline will become an obstruction to the development of disciplined people.

1387. If difficulties will come to disciplined people, those will make them powerful.

1388. Thoughts have to change first to develop. Later, words and then, deeds have to change.

1389. People who have no patience cannot identify superior things. People who do not have endurance cannot get superior things. People who do not work hard cannot become good people. People who do not exert themselves cannot do the best things.

-13-

Strength, Weakness

1390. Those who love themselves can identify their abilities, strengths and weaknesses.

1391. Those who adopt strengths become strong. Those who adopt weaknesses become weak.

1392. Weakest persons in human beings:

    1. Make others responsible for their mistakes.

    2. Blame others to cover their own mistakes.

1393. Those who accept weaknesses will have to uphold others and become strong. Those who cover their weaknesses will lose and become weaker.

1394. Weakness leads to search.

1395. People who lose are not weak; weak are those who cannot earn.

1396. One should call those who cannot see as they're not able to see. Those who don't understand by seeing, and cannot grasp by listening must be called a mentally weak person.

1397. If a person is to be made the best, his strength is known. If a person wanted to be used, his weakness is known. It depends on the way of seeing the person.

1398. People who do not know are not incapable. Those who cannot know are incapable.

    Weak are those who do not do it even after knowing. Powerless are those who cannot do even after knowing.

1399. The people who can bear and eliminate the losses can forgive those who cause losses.

The people who cannot bear, or eliminate the losses cannot forgive those who cause losses.

1400. If more members are there, the more the strength to the family. If many members are unemployed the more miserable will be the family.

1401. There is no place for ignorance, slavery, weakness, insult, defeat, and cowardice where there is self-respect and self-confidence.

1402. Those who lose self-respect and people for their needs are – weak, worthless and worse people.

1403. Every strong thing will be weak when impeded by a strong thing.

1404. Very weak are those who cheat themselves.

1405. Psychologically weak people cannot understand others.

1406. Strong people forgive honestly. Those who ask for forgiveness honestly are strong.

1407. A weak person tries to weaken others. A strong person tries to make others strong.

1408. Those who think that whatever happens is for our good are weak. Those who think that what happened is good or bad are wise. Those who convert the bad into good are believers.

-14-

War, Struggle, Revolution

1409. Doing even when there is a need or no need is war. Doing in unavoidable circumstances is fighting.

1410. If done for dominance, it will be war. If done for protection and rights it will be fighting.

1411. There may or may not be ethics in war. But there will be ethics in fighting.

1412. Fighting is greater than war.

1413. A fighter is always valuable. If he is a winner, he is a warrior; if he is a loser, he is a hero.

1414. The aim of fighting is not to win; it is about not compromising.

1415. People who are born to kings get formality, but cannot get war by birth. War has to be learned.

1416. People who learn war gain kingdoms. But not to people who have formality.

1417. Learning war is enough to win an enemy. But to escape from detractors, sometimes, one should leave the terms.

1418. It is easy to identify enemies but identifying detractors is difficult.

1419. Enemies can become friends, but detractors cannot become friends.

1420. Revolution will not be born in the same way in the same society.

1421. Reason for revolution – self-respect. Reason for success – self-confidence.

1422. If you do it for yourself – fight. If you do it for others – revolution.

1423. Revolution can be born in a society anytime and in any way.

-15-

Suicide

1424. If a person kills his own body, it should not be called suicide. It should be called a sacrifice of body, a sacrifice of life.

1425. Those who cannot live against their likes and their soul sacrifice their bodies and life. The world calls them cowards and people who committed suicide.

1426. It is possible to live by separating the soul. A few people live like this in this world.

-16-

Change

1427. No change is possible without an alternative.

1428. Time is needed for any change to happen. If time is not given for the change, change is not possible.

1429. Those who want to change and who want to change others must have patience, endurance and forgiveness.

1430. A generation that did not change means:

    1. A generation that has not developed.

    2. No chances for the next generation to get developed.

1431. It is wrong to not give a chance to change. It is sin that is not changed when a chance is given.

1432. The people who have arrogance cannot change.

1433. Those who pretend as changed can never change.

1434. Those who pretend as changed will lose the change.

1435. One person will not change if someone asked to change. One person can change only when their situation is also changed.

1436. Change is moving from one level to another level. Change is not the opposite aspect.

-17-

Other Sentences

1437. The name given by a selfish person to the virtue of sharing with others is coy.

1438. People who do not know about forgiveness give the name weakness to it.

1439. People who do not know the meaning of sacrifice call it getting cheated.

1440. Bad people give the name to incapable and too good-natured people.

1441. The names were given to a believer by weak and unfaithful persons: liar, boastful.

1442. The names given to things that cannot be understood or done are mad things or great things.

1443. People who do not have and expect from others are implored people.

Those who expect from others even if they have are beggars.

1444. The greatest language in this world, the invisible language – the language to understand by heart.

1445. Food donation is of two types:

1. Feeding a needy person many times.
2. Feeding many needy persons.

1446. Two types of human beings:

1. Those who are happy by harming others.
2. Those who are happy by doing good to others.

1447. Two types of human beings are:

1. Those who try to be good.

2. Those who pretend to be good.

1448. Two types of human beings:

1. Learners.

2. Jealous people.

1449. Two types of human beings:

1. Wise people.

2. Ignorant people.

1450. Two types of human beings:

1. Those who love.

2. Those who hate.

1451. Two types of human beings:

1. Honest people.

2. Corrupt people.

1452. Diversity is not the opposite.

1453. All elders cannot be gentlemen.

1454. Histories can become writing. Writings become histories.

1455. Illicit spreads where there is no order.

1456. Those who disobey orders deserve punishment.

1457. Whatever gives light stays at a height.

1458. Humans can only destroy things that get destroyed.

1459. People who have no life give more value to lifeless aspects.

1460. Politics cannot change students, but students can change politics.

1461. The person who donates to get noticed by all is like a cloud that does not rain.

1462. Those who have gratitude keep hatred away.

1463. Those who follow orders receive promises.

1464. No person has authority over anything that does not belong to him.

1465. Impatient people cannot have discernment. They have no discretion.

1466. Opportunism of one person can lead to the opportunism of another person.

1467. Those who want only their well-being might be good, but they can never become great.

1468. All are the same when sleeping, we know who is who when they get up.

1469. Those who do not have a conscience will have arrogance.

1470. Wrongs made for lack of food are mistakes.

1471. Humans cannot pollute nature; depending on the illicit acts of humans, nature pollutes humans.

1472. A person can know himself and others also know about him when he has nothing.

1473. Opportunities are around everyone. But only able persons can see them.

1474. People can change to new clothes and food immediately. But cannot change to new thoughts immediately.

1475. Human beings get influenced early by visible things, but cannot be influenced early by invisible things.

1476. Those which change according to region and situations are not truths, virtues or theories; they become limitations, needs and restrictions.

-18-

Society – People

1477. Not all people in society are alike:

1. Exemplary people – Finest people.
2. Mediocre people – Intermediate people.
3. Sub-minimal people – Wicked people.
4. Sinner people – Vile people.

1478. **Exemplary people – Finest people:**

These people live in reality with ethics. They help others and society. They seek and do good to others and have a personality of love, kindness, mercy, sacrifice and courage. These people live ideally as pioneers. These people have the knowledge, suffer for others, uphold poor and weak people, and do service to others; these people follow truth and have purity, compassion and humility. These people also follow justice and virtue and live for a purpose.

1479. **Mediocre people – Intermediate people:**

These people live for themselves and depend on their hard work. These people do not harm society but are useful by offering service. These people live by doing work or profession in the existence of society. These people do not depend on others; have comforts and problems, and live with satisfaction. These people will help others and offer donations. These people utilize time correctly and have respect and fear for society and elders. These people live by focusing on education, intelligence, money, employment and relations. These people give value to others, are obedient, correct their mistakes, and give value to belief. These people have discipline, gratitude and goal.

1480. **Sub-minimal people – Wicked people:**

These people depend on others, utilize most of their time for eating, sleeping and comfort and live only for comfort. These people do not want to work hard and are sluggish and lazy, and they waste their time. These people become slaves to money, intoxication and power. These people will forget the good done to them and blame others for their jealousy and hate, and not act with responsibility. These people are selfish, sit idly, and they do not know why they are living. These people have cowardice and greed. These people behave differently before and at the back of others. These people are cheaters and degraded persons, and they make fun of others and show partiality. These people do not understand others and look down upon lowly, poor, elderly people and disabled persons. These people make fake promises and justify their mistakes. They will depend on lies and create problems for others for their needs. These people are promiscuous and have hatred, negligence and stupidity They don't have obedience and gratitude.

1481. **Sinner people – Vile people:-**

These people make wrong judgments, give false evidence and repeatedly commit mistakes along with being corrupt, unjust, unrighteous, illegal, and treacherous. These people will justify their mistakes, harm people who helped them, kill others for their own advantage, and cheat themselves and others. These people will insult others and cheat society. These people's behaviour is totally in contrast to their words and deeds. And they have no pity for others. These people create and preach wrong sentences, paths and theories, which are against moral values. These people will deceive others for their own advantage and make them slaves. They will enjoy seeing the problems and difficulties of others. These people will conspire, betray, cheat and kill others.

1482. **Sinner people, vile people and sub-minimal people, wicked people can transform into Exemplary people, finest people and mediocre people, intermediate people.**

Truth Always Wins

Assisted People

1. New Hope Ministries and Members,
Mr. M. M. Surendrababu, (Founder and Pastor)
A. Mallikhaarjun, (Assistant).
New Hope Evangelical Church,
H.no: 3-141, Plot no: 36,
Santhinagar, Vanasthalipuram,
Hyderabad, Telangana,
Pin: 500070.

2. Mr. Subbarayudu Gali, (Ex. APSRTC), (Ex. MPTC) Family,
Brahmanayudu (Beliver)
Karumanchi (village), Tanguturu (Mandal),
Prakasam (Dist.), Andhra Pradesh,
India, Pin: 523272.

For suggestions and doubts; abhisheak1239@gmail.com

www.ingramcontent.com/pod-product-compliance
Lightning Source LLC
LaVergne TN
LVHW050548160826
845677LV00011B/2233

* 9 7 9 8 8 8 8 6 9 3 3 8 4 *